COPING WITH ANX

D1101959

SHIRLEY TRICKETT
becoming a counsellor and teacher. She has worked with
anxious and depressed people for several years, and is
the author of the successful *Coming off Tranquillizers*
(1987). In 1987 she won a Whitbread Community Care
Award.

01
97

Overcoming Common Problems Series

Beating Job Burnout
DR DONALD SCOTT

Beating the Blues
SUSAN TANNER AND JILLIAN BALL

Being the Boss
STEPHEN FITZSIMON

Birth Over Thirty
SHEILA KITZINGER

Body Language
How to read others' thoughts by their gestures
ALLAN PEASE

Bodypower
DR VERNON COLEMAN

Bodysense
DR VERNON COLEMAN

Calm Down
How to cope with frustration and anger
DR PAUL HAUCK

Comfort for Depression
JANET HORWOOD

Common Childhood Illnesses
DR PATRICIA GILBERT

Complete Public Speaker
GYLES BRANDRETH

Coping Successfully with Your Child's Asthma
DR PAUL CARSON

Coping Successfully with Your Child's Skin Problems
DR PAUL CARSON

Coping Successfully with Your Hyperactive Child
DR PAUL CARSON

Coping Successfully with Your Irritable Bowel
ROSEMARY NICOL

Coping with Anxiety and Depression
SHIRLEY TRICKETT

Coping with Cot Death
SARAH MURPHY

Coping with Depression and Elation
DR PATRICK McKEON

Coping with Stress
DR GEORGIA WITKIN-LANOIL

Coping with Suicide
DR DONALD SCOTT

Coping with Thrush
CAROLINE CLAYTON

Curing Arthritis – The Drug-Free Way
MARGARET HILLS

Curing Arthritis Diet Book
MARGARET HILLS

Curing Coughs, Colds and Flu – The Drug-Free Way
MARGARET HILLS

Curing Illness – The Drug-Free Way
MARGARET HILLS

Depression
DR PAUL HAUCK

Divorce and Separation
ANGELA WILLANS

The Dr Moerman Cancer Diet
RUTH JOCHEMS

The Epilepsy Handbook
SHELAGH McGOVERN

Everything You Need to Know about Adoption
MAGGIE JONES

Everything You Need to Know about Contact Lenses
DR ROBERT YOUNGSON

Everything You Need to Know about Osteoporosis
ROSEMARY NICOL

Everything You Need to Know about Shingles
DR ROBERT YOUNGSON

Everything You Need to Know about Your Eyes
DR ROBERT YOUNGSON

Family First Aid and Emergency Handbook
DR ANDREW STANWAY

Overcoming Common Problems Series

Feverfew
A traditional herbal remedy for migraine and arthritis
DR STEWART JOHNSON

Fight Your Phobia and Win
DAVID LEWIS

Getting Along with People
DIANNE DOUBTFIRE

Goodbye Backache
DR DAVID IMRIE WITH COLLEEN DIMSON

Helping Children Cope with Divorce
ROSEMARY WELLS

Helping Children Cope with Grief
ROSEMARY WELLS

How to be a Successful Secretary
SUE DYSON AND STEPHEN HOARE

How to Be Your Own Best Friend
DR PAUL HAUCK

How to Control your Drinking
DRS W. MILLER AND R. MUNOZ

How to Cope with Stress
DR PETER TYRER

How to Cope with Tinnitus and Hearing Loss
DR ROBERT YOUNGSON

How to Cope with Your Child's Allergies
DR PAUL CARSON

How to Cure Your Ulcer
ANNE CHARLISH AND DR BRIAN GAZZARD

How to Do What You Want to Do
DR PAUL HAUCK

How to Enjoy Your Old Age
DR B. F. SKINNER AND M. E. VAUGHAN

How to Get Things Done
ALISON HARDINGHAM

How to Improve Your Confidence
DR KENNETH HAMBLY

How to Interview and Be Interviewed
MICHELE BROWN AND GYLES BRANDRETH

How to Love a Difficult Man
NANCY GOOD

How to Love and be Loved
DR PAUL HAUCK

How to Make Successful Decisions
ALISON HARDINGHAM

How to Move House Successfully
ANNE CHARLISH

How to Pass Your Driving Test
DONALD RIDLAND

How to Say No to Alcohol
KEITH McNEILL

How to Spot Your Child's Potential
CECILE DROUIN AND ALAIN DUBOS

How to Stand up for Yourself
DR PAUL HAUCK

How to Start a Conversation and Make Friends
DON GABOR

How to Stop Feeling Guilty
DR VERNON COLEMAN

How to Stop Smoking
GEORGE TARGET

How to Stop Taking Tranquillisers
DR PETER TYRER

How to Stop Worrying
DR FRANK TALLIS

Hysterectomy
SUZIE HAYMAN

If Your Child is Diabetic
JOANNE ELLIOTT

Jealousy
DR PAUL HAUCK

Learning to Live with Multiple Sclerosis
DR ROBERT POVEY. ROBIN DOWIE AND GILLIAN PRETT

Overcoming Common Problems Series

Living Alone – A Woman's Guide
LIZ McNEILL TAYLOR

Living Through Personal Crisis
ANN KAISER STEARNS

Living with Grief
DR TONY LAKE

Living with High Blood Pressure
DR TOM SMITH

Loneliness
DR TONY LAKE

Making Marriage Work
DR PAUL HAUCK

Making the Most of Loving
GILL COX AND SHEILA DAINOW

Making the Most of Yourself
GILL COX AND SHEILA DAINOW

Managing Two Careers
How to survive as a working mother
PATRICIA O'BRIEN

Meeting People is Fun
How to overcome shyness
DR PHYLLIS SHAW

Menopause
RAEWYN MACKENZIE

The Nervous Person's Companion
DR KENNETH HAMBLY

Overcoming Fears and Phobias
DR TONY WHITEHEAD

Overcoming Shyness
A woman's guide
DIANNE DOUBTFIRE

Overcoming Stress
DR VERNON COLEMAN

Overcoming Tension
DR KENNETH HAMBLY

Overcoming Your Nerves
DR TONY LAKE

The Parkinson's Disease Handbook
DR RICHARD GODWIN-AUSTEN

Say When!
Everything a woman needs to know about
alcohol and drinking problems
ROSEMARY KENT

Self-Help for your Arthritis
EDNA PEMBLE

Sleep Like a Dream – The Drug-Free Way
ROSEMARY NICOL

Solving your Personal Problems
PETER HONEY

Someone to Love
How to find romance in the personal columns
MARGARET NELSON

A Special Child in the Family
Living with your sick or disabled child
DIANA KIMPTON

Stress and your Stomach
DR VERNON COLEMAN

Think Your Way to Happiness
DR WINDY DRYDEN AND JACK GORDON

Trying to Have a Baby?
Overcoming infertility and child loss
MAGGIE JONES

What Everyone Should Know about Drugs
KENNETH LEECH

Why Be Afraid?
How to overcome your fears
DR PAUL HAUCK

Women and Depression
A practical self-help guide
DEIDRE SANDERS

You and Your Varicose Veins
DR PATRICIA GILBERT

Your Arthritic Hip and You
GEORGE TARGET

Overcoming Common Problems

COPING WITH
ANXIETY AND DEPRESSION

Shirley Trickett

SHELDON PRESS
LONDON

First published in Great Britain 1989
Sheldon Press, SPCK, Marylebone Road, London NW1 4DU

Second impression 1990

© Shirley Trickett 1989

British Library Cataloguing in Publication Data
Trickett, Shirley
   Coping with anxiety and depression
   1. Man. Neuroses. Anxiety.   2. Man. Psychoses.
   Depression
   I. Title   II. Series
   616.85′223

   ISBN 0–85969–592–1

Typeset by Detatype Ltd, Ellesmere Port, Cheshire
Printed and bound in Great Britain by
Courier International Ltd, Tiptree, Essex

For my children, Helen, David and Sarah, who love me in spite of being on the receiving end of all my inexperience.

Contents

Foreword *by Dr J W McDonald*   xi

PART ONE: *Understanding Anxiety and Depression*

1   Anxiety, Depression and the Whole Person   3
2   What is Anxiety? What is Depression?   6
3   Understanding the Nervous System   9
4   How to Get off the Speed Track   12
5   Learn More About Your Nerves   14
6   Causes of Exhausted Nerves   27
7   Learning to Be Yourself – Be Real   32
8   Understanding the Nature of Anxiety   37
9   Understanding the Nature of Depression   41
10 What is a Nervous Breakdown?   49
11 Drug and Non-Drug Treatments for Depression
    and Anxiety   55
12 Physical Reasons for Anxiety and Depression   60
13 Misdiagnosis   68

PART TWO: *Self-help Therapy for Anxiety and Depression*

14 Being Your Own Therapist   73
15 Working with Your Body – Relaxation   78
16 Hyperventilation   89

17 Hypoglycaemia (Low Blood Sugar) and Nerves   94

18 Quick References to Combat Depression
    and Anxiety   105

    PART THREE: *What About the Spirit?*

19 What About the Spirit?   109

    Books, tapes and further information   112
    Index   114

Foreword

When I first met Shirley Trickett I was at medical school, learning that tranquillizers were an effective, safe and non-addictive treatment for anxiety. Of course, like any good medical student, I believed it. When Shirley told me that she thought that these drugs were addictive I was naturally rather sceptical and said, politely, that the medical world might listen when she had hard evidence to prove her case. Far from being discouraged by the indifference of the medical profession, not to mention jumped-up medical students, she set about gathering that evidence, while at the same time getting on with the job of helping people to deal with their problems in ways other than taking drugs. She has been instrumental in a campaign which has alerted doctors to the dangers of tranquillizers and, in the process, she has acquired an expertise in the management of anxiety problems which is second to none.

Some years have passed since Shirley first bent my ear about tranquillizers and a new generation of medical students is learning that tranquillizers are dangerous, addictive and ineffective in the treatment of anxiety. Her opinions, once medical heresy, have become medical fact. Her first book, *Coming off Tranquillizers and Sleeping Pills*, has become essential reading not just for those trying to find a new life without drugs like Ativan and Valium, but also for doctors like myself, who have to deal with such problems in the course of their work. I regularly recommend Shirley's first book to my patients when they ask about tranquillizer addiction, and their reaction is usually: 'This is amazing, Doctor, I could have written it myself. It's *exactly* how I feel.'

Now that tranquillizers have fallen from favour and the medical profession is trying to undo the damage of twenty years mistakenly prescribing them, we have found ourselves with little alternative treatment to offer patients suffering from anxiety or 'milder' forms of depression. Fortunately, while we had been seeking chemical answers to emotional problems and encouraging patients to believe these were possible, people like Shirley had been looking for other ways of dealing with anxiety and depression. This hard-earned knowledge is now finding its way into psychiatric practice with good effect. More importantly, we are now seeing a climate emerging in which people are showing a greater interest in their psychological welfare and a greater willingness to seek the solution to their problems on their own or in self-help groups.

This book, written with the clarity and insight which made *Coming off Tranquillizers and Sleeping Pills* such a great success, tackles the problems of anxiety and depression with a compassion that springs from first-hand experience and an expertise which has come from a receptiveness to new ideas which my own profession would do well to learn from. I am sure that *Coping with Anxiety and Depression* will take its place alongside *Coming Off Tranquillizers* in offering hope to those who suffer from the misery of these conditions and at the same time providing excellent practical guidance to health care professionals working in this field.

Dr J. W. McDonald,
Registrar in Psychiatry
Rainhill Hospital
Prescott
Merseyside

PART ONE
Understanding Anxiety and Depression

1

Anxiety, Depression and the Whole Person

Since the publication of *Coming off Tranquillizers and Sleeping Pills* I have had many requests to write more about anxiety and depression. The National Health Service provides treatment for people suffering from severe psychiatric disorders but does very little for what is considered to be less severe nervous illness: mild to moderate states of anxiety and depression. This may be the way these conditions are described, but there is rarely anything mild or moderate about the degree of misery involved. The symptoms are often severe, protracted and very frightening. I hope that what follows in this book will help and encourage those who feel defeated and degraded by nervous troubles.

The conventional approach to the nervously ill so often fails because only part of the person is looked at. Unless body, mind and spirit are all nurtured, full recovery cannot take place. Homing in on just one problem is like painting the same section of the Forth Bridge over and over again. No matter how much the paint gleams in the treated part, it will not stop rust developing elsewhere, making the whole structure unstable.

As medicine gets more and more specialized it seems to retreat from the all-round commonsense approach of the old days. We are losing something very valuable here. Each professional 'hat' is firmly tied on and the therapist does not see anything outside his/her discipline. Take Mary, for example: she is seeing her psychiatrist regularly, she finds him helpful, but would make much better progress if only he would open his eyes and see her physical needs too. She is always covered in herpes (cold sores) and is painfully thin. He is so bound up in her neurosis that he does not see the rest.

3

This happens in all areas of medicine. When the nurse visits John, she is so busy dressing his leg and filling him full of antibiotics, she does not see how much he is grieving for his wife. Are Richard's needs really being met? His death phobia will not respond to tranquillizers; he needs a loving dose of hope *and* to be taught how much he is damaging his nerves by his hectic daily routine.

This book is for the nervous person as a whole: aching body, confused mind and wearied spirit. Its goal is to explain in a simple way some of the causes of anxiety and depression, and by discussing the symptoms help you to identify whether it is anxiety or depression or a mixture of the two that is making you feel so ill.

It also stresses the importance of learning to love and accept yourself just as you are and realize there is no shame or blame attached to being nervously ill – it can happen to anyone. The nervous system is not separate – somewhere outside the body – it's right in there with the bones, muscles, skin etc. If your body or mind has more stress than it can take then it hurts your nerves. It's as simple as that.

Part One deals with understanding the causes and problems in anxiety and depression, and their treatments, both medicinal and non-medicinal. Part Two, the self-help section, shows how you can work *with* your body instead of pushing against it. Self-help can also work very well with medical help. They do not exclude each other. Many doctors encourage people to seek information and be more responsible about their nerves.

Although there are many words used for nervous illness – affective disorder, anxiety, depression, mood disorder, neurosis, nervous breakdown etc. – it all comes back to the same thing; tired nerves – and tired nerves can recover, if they are given the chance.

No matter how long you have been nervously ill, you can recover and find peace and joy in life. Be prepared to accept that it will take time, and that there will be ups and downs — nature does not heal in a straight line.

While the symptoms on the following pages may be only too familiar and seem unimportant, all persistent symptoms must be investigated. Consult your doctor if you have not already done so. If you are told 'It's only your nerves', then self-help could change your life.

2
What is Anxiety?
What is Depression?

What is total health?

True health is not just absence of symptoms, it is characterized by feeling physically well, being self-reliant, having
the ability to adjust to change, and having a sense of
responsibility for oneself. This entails developing insight into
one's own feelings and actions, and cultivating a degree of
self-worth that can stand on its own without the good opinion
of others.

What is nervous illness?

The most common symptoms of nervous illness are anxiety
and depression, conditions that can occur alone or together.
The feelings they produce range from mild tension or being
'down', to symptoms so disabling that a normal life is not
possible.

What is anxiety?

The word *anxiety* comes from a Latin word meaning 'worried
about the unknown', and is also related to a Greek word
meaning 'compress or strangle'. Are you being strangled by
anxiety? Anxiety is a reaction to living in the world. It is as
much part of our world as eating. It has been here since man
began. *It is normal.* How can we escape it, since it starts with
the trauma of birth?

6

Let us daydream

If it were possible to be conceived with love, in a clean trouble-free environment, and to spend our days *in utero* happily splashing around in a serene, well-nourished mother, this would be a good start for a trouble-free journey. If it were also possible to slide painlessly through the birth canal to arrive in a gentle world, free from harsh lights and noises that assault our senses; and if we were received into warm water and not up-ended by buttock-slapping hands (the first injustice!) this would be another step in the right direction.

And if we held a guarantee from God, saying, 'You will be loved with a love that sets you free; you will be disciplined with gentleness and, after long years of happiness and fulfilment, you will leave this life as painlessly as you entered it,' *then anxiety would not be normal*.

You can see it is impossible not to have *some* degree of anxiety. The aim is not to fight fear continually, but to live happily alongside it by learning how to reduce it to manageable proportions. If you are ashamed of being anxious, then you are ashamed of being a human being and having a body. We experience the world through our bodies.

Is anxiety necesssary?

When we are afraid, chemical changes in our bodies take place that increase the energy levels and enable us to respond to the danger or stress (fight or flight) – for example, running from a charging bull, or staying up late to study for exams. The trouble starts when we cannot switch off this extra energy when it is no longer needed; the body fails to adjust and we become 'wound up'. This useless state is rather like leaving the car engine running for 24 hours when you only need it running for two short journeys daily. In the same way as the petrol is wasted and runs out, our energy is wasted, our nervous system is depleted, and we eventually become ill.

What is depression?

Depression is an illness of the *feelings*. It ranges from an overreaction to normal sadness, to grey nothingness where you are still just able to function, to utter despair, hopelessness and prostration. In severe depression even the bodily functions are affected.

Is depression necessary?

In anxiety activity of body and mind are *speeded up*. In depression they are *slowed down*. Depression often follows anxiety – it forces us to rest; this could be its function. Although this slowing down can be useful, if it goes on too long you need to do something about it.

It will be easier to understand how we become anxious and depressed if you first learn how the nervous system works. This we deal with in the next chapter.

3

Understanding the Nervous System

The nervous system is the network of communication between various parts of the body rather like a telephone exchange with the brain as the central switchboard, the spine as the main cable, and the nerves as the telephone lines that carry messages. It is divided into two systems: the central and autonomic. .

The central nervous system

This controls voluntary movement and is responsible for all sensations in muscles, bones and joints. It is under the control of the *will* – you want to pick up a pen, you reach out your hand and do so. This system works well unless it is neurologically impaired or, in times of terror, paralysed with fear.

The autonomic nervous system

The autonomic nervous system controls all involuntary muscles – internal organs, blood vessels, etc. This system is under the control of the emotions; for example, anger will cause your blood pressure to rise, fear will make the stomach churn. It has two parts: the *sympathetic*, which has a stimulating effect; and the *parasympathetic*, which has a calming effect.

When your parasympathetic nervous system does not work properly you become overanxious.

Think of the *sympathetic nervous system* as the man in a red Ferrari speeding along with his foot hard down on the accelerator pedal, fast. Think of the *parasympathetic nervous system* as the man pottering around in a blue Morris Minor, slowly. All the internal organs have two sets of nerves, one stimulating, the other quietening.

The sympathetic nervous system – go, go, go

Imagine a fireman going to fight a fire. His nervous system is 'sympathetic' to his emotions and prepares his body to fight for survival. It does this in response to him *tightening* his muscles and squeezing his glands and, rather like squeezing oranges, it produces 'juice', a chemical called *adrenalin*. As a result, his blood pressure rises, his heart rate speeds up, his breathing becomes rapid (he needs more oxygen because he is rushing around) and he sweats to cool himself. To help him even more, his blood is diverted from his abdomen to his legs so that he can run faster. (This is the reason for that sinking feeling in the stomach when we are afraid.) With a reduced blood supply to his digestive organs he does not think of food, or of the need to go to the lavatory. So when his sympathetic nervous system is in action: *his adrenalin/anxiety levels are high*.

Do you see that his body is behaving very much like that of an overanxious person, with rapid breathing and pulse, sweating etc. The difference is he is using his anxiety *productively*, and there *is* something to worry about. If he had been very fearful and had not used the extra adrenalin he could have become so tense that he vomited and emptied the contents of his bowel and bladder (shit-scared). This may be a primitive mechanism for making the body lighter to enable it to run faster.

How does the fireman get back to normal adrenalin levels? When the fire is out the danger is over, the fireman sits in the van on the way back to the station, and *when he relaxes his tight muslces* different chemicals are released to give the opposite effect to adrenalin. This is the parasympathetic system working efficiently: his blood pressure drops, his heart rate and breathing slow down, he stops sweating, the blood comes back into his abdomen from his arms and legs – he realizes he is hungry, and starts thinking about food. He is also conscious that he needs the lavatory. He feels relaxed, his muscles are comfortable. So *his adrenalin/anxiety levels are low*.

It is easy to see from this why the nerves get exhausted. Repeated stresses, conscious and unconscious (even small ones), keep us in a state of red alert all the time. It's like the fireman rushing around with buckets of water long after the fire is out. He wants to slow down but he can't. His adrenalin (and therefore anxiety) levels are still too high.

Have you ever been so wound up that you carried on working long after you needed to even though you were exhausted? Chapter 4 tells you how to slow down and get off the speed track.

4

How to Get off the Speed Track

Working with the parasympathetic nervous system

Since this slowing down part of the nervous system responds to the emotions, it would seem sensible to say to yourself: there is absolutely nothing to make me so fearful – calm down, stop sending out so much adrenalin, I don't need it. Unfortunately a brain flooded with adrenalin does not listen to reason, it is obeying the chemical messengers which are telling it to speed up. The best first aid treatment is to use the body to calm down. You can eventually train your body to obey your commands anywhere you are. Self-talk is very useful in the long term, but in the panic situation it is not very effective. You need to do *mechanically* what your parasympathetic (the slow one) should be doing *automatically*. It is rather like having to crank start a car when the ignition fails. Your relaxation response needs an MOT.

Remember what made the fireman relax

If the muscles relax then the chain reaction for the relaxation response is set in motion. You may not be able to do this at will because you are so uptight, but by slowing down your breathing you can reduce the amount of oxygen getting to your brain, and coax your parasympathetic to take over. This is fully described later.

I can't be bothered with this – I want an instant cure

Some anxious people get irritated when it is suggested that they can train their bodies not to be on 'red alert' all the time. They want an instant cure for the dreadful feelings of panic – a pill or an injection They often get annoyed when it is suggested that their bodies are responsible for the feelings.

12

They prefer to think the 'wobblies' descend 'out of nowhere' and have nothing to do with them at all.

The truth is they have no conscious part in it, but fail to realize their symptoms are caused by the nervous system being weakened by repeated strain, not only from the present life situation, but also from the stored pain in the unconscious. (When pain is mentioned in this book it will mean emotional pain: sadness, grief, anger, frustration, loneliness etc. unless physical pain is specifically mentioned.)

Happily, most people are eager to learn how to use their bodies in a way that will allow the nerves to heal. Confidence grows as they feel the results. Many say: 'My life is still full of problems, but I can feel my body is reacting differently now.'

It's worth the effort

Are you willing to be bullied by your unconscious into using tension to enable you to cope with stress, or are you willing to enrol in the 'get on better with your nerves school', and do the boring work necessary to feel more in charge?

The methods described in this book are safe, cheap and effective. They are also sometimes a bind and time-consuming! Some people have said that it feels like self-absorption to be continually watching yourself. But it is really self-interest, used productively as a means to an end. It is better to be absorbed in the *cure* than the symptoms. Anxious or depressed people are the first to admit anyway that they are preoccupied with their symptoms all the time.

5

Learn More About Your Nerves

What are nervous symptoms?

Feeling constantly exhausted
No interest in life
Panic
Irritability
Lack of concentration
Attention-seeking
Hyperactivity
Rapid speech
Rapid thoughts
Compulsive eating
Paranoia
Phobias
Feelings of gloom and doom
Suicidal feelings
Restlessness
Crying easily
Compulsions,
Obsessions
Impotence, loss of interest in sex
Tight chest or throat
Shaking
Dizziness
Diarrhoea
Wind
Insomnia
Breathing difficulties
Bumping heart
Excessive sweating
Swallowing problems
Loss of appetite and weight
Headaches
Tinnitus (ringing in the ears)
Aching all over

There are several responses to a list of nervous symptoms. The most common one is: I was pleased to see all those things written down – I thought I was imagining them. Because people are often pessimistic when their nerves are in trouble, sometimes they cry: 'Oh dear, I have so many of the symptoms on this list I must be having a breakdown.' But if they could change it to: 'I have quite a few of these symptoms, it is time I took more care of myself', they would make a much speedier recovery. Worrying over the symptoms can perpetuate the illness.

What does it feel like to be overanxious?

Because the whole body is stimulated *everything* is speeded up. This can result in: an increase in movement; thoughts being multiplied alarmingly, incessant and rapid speech; and also a speeding up of many of the functions of the body, such as heart-rate, breathing and the rate at which food and fluid go through the digestive tract. Hence the need to go to the lavatory so often.

With all this to cope with it is not surprising that the behaviour of the person who has become overanxious changes. Relatives become very upset when the person they know as loving and easygoing becomes irritable, suspicious and generally exhausting to be with. But it must be remembered that sufferers are not *choosing* this behaviour and are often also bewildered and frightened by their angry and sometimes evil thoughts, and the thoughtless actions they are inflicting on those they love.

In the rest of this chapter we explain some of the most distressing of these symptoms and what causes them.

Feelings of gloom and doom

All the feelings caused by being overanxious are unpleasant, but the hardest to cope with are the wayward thoughts that become distorted and gloomy. For example, when you are well, if your husband is five minutes late home from work you would think he was held up in the traffic; when you are overanxious you are convinced he is lying injured under a ten tonne truck. Health phobias are also very common. Every minor disorder is thought to be cancer. It can also turn an uneasy feeling into a fullblown panic attack. For example, normally when you are in a crowded place you might think, 'I will be glad to get out of here'. When you are overanxious you can become terror-stricken in the same situation and be convinced you are seriously ill, 'I must get home, I am going to die/be sick/lose control', etc. Panic attacks and how to cope with them are discussed below.

Suicidal feelings

*When anxiety levels are very high it is common to have suicidal feelings. These usually disappear as the anxiety levels come down, but it is **essential** to see your doctor if you are having this experience.* The Samaritans are always there and ready to help. Do not hesitate to contact them even if you know you would not act on the feelings. Many people say: 'I had these awful suicidal feelings but I did not feel I could ring the Samaritans because I knew I would not do anything. I feel so ashamed of these feelings; I have a lovely wife/husband and family and cannot see any reason for the way I feel.' The operator will give you the number if you can't concentrate enough to find it in the book.

It's my agoraphobia – it's my panic attacks

Sometimes people see suicidal feelings, panic attacks or agoraphobia (fear of being out, particularly alone) as an illness in itself. It often takes a lot to convince them that although it may be the worst effect they are experiencing it is only part of the story and will go as the anxiety levels come down. It is rather like seeing the cough in someone with bronchitis as the illness itself; the cough would not be there if the lungs were not congested. In the same way, the panic, agoraphobia etc. would not be there if the anxiety (adrenalin) levels were normal.

Panic attacks

Even reading about panic attacks makes some people feel nervous, so do remember that you might be causing yours by simply going too long without food or breathing badly. More about this in Chapters 16 and 17.

Panic attacks are characterized by sudden intense feelings of anxiety often associated with feelings of impending death or disaster and fear of going mad. Unpleasant physical feelings are also present including:

palpitations
dizziness
nausea
shaking
choking sensations
feelings of unreality
an urgent need for the lavatory
hot and cold flushes
pins and needles

The attacks can last seconds or minutes or, more rarely, hours. In many ways a panic attack is *worse* than being in a frightening situation; at least in the latter you know what the danger is, and when it is over feel relief, and presumably know how to avoid getting into that situation again. In a panic attack you are afraid of the feelings and even more afraid of the cause because you *don't know what it is*. That is why most people think they are seriously ill or even that it is the end of the world. Fear of the fear takes over.

Are panic attacks a danger to your health?

Panic attacks are not a danger to your health and once you recognize them for what they are – just a flood of adrenalin that makes you feel awful – they can be knocked down to size and conquered. What causes panic and how to cope with it is described on page 92.

When do panic attacks happen?

Here are three typical examples.

I was sitting reading when I was gripped with the most

awful feeling – a mixture of fear and sadness. I had never experienced anything like it before. The urge to move was overwhelming and I started to pace about the room. My wife tried to reassure me by saying it was only exhaustion. I felt quite irritated; such dreadful feelings could only be a stroke or heart attack. It completely obliterated my normal reactions; I could see I was alarming her but felt no concern. It passed off after a few minutes, but the fear of it happening again lingered for several days. I felt better when my wife's friend gave me a cutting from a magazine. It said if you were run down and missed meals you could have a panic attack and it described exactly what I had felt. On the day it happened I had worked through lunch with only a cup of coffee and Ann was about to serve dinner when the feelings started.

The first one came when I was in the supermarket. I was reaching for an orange when the most awful feeling came over me; it was a mixture of a feeling of terrible loss and fear that something was going to happen. Everything seemed unreal. Fear of losing control overwhelmed me – I felt hot and sick and my legs were like jelly. I left the full shopping trolley and rushed home. It only lasted a few minutes. I felt such a fool when I thought about the shopping. The next couple of days were a bit dreary and then I seemed fine. It happened again two weeks later in the library. Eventually I had to go to the doctor because I became afraid to go out alone. My husband had to take me to work in the car and I took a taxi home. I told my colleagues my back was troubling me.

The doctor said my nerves were worn out and I must take two weeks sick-leave. He knew me well enough to say I was not to use the time to build a rockery or paint the house. I have had a very stressful life, but have always seen myself as having nerves of steel – a coper.

18

I felt quite affronted when I left the surgery with a sick note, diet sheet (I had been doing a lot of 'comfort' eating) and orders to rest and reorganize my life into a quieter routine. He scared me into following his instructions by saying if I did not slow down I could have a nervous breakdown – me! I thought, only thin, twittery people have breakdowns.

I can see now there was part of me that was afraid to stop. Rushing around, prevented me from looking at what was going on inside. There was also the fear; if I stop perhaps I won't be able to get started again. It reminded me of when my son was young. We had walked the long way home. I asked him if he would like to sit on the grass for a rest. His reply was, 'No, Mummy, all the tiredness will come out and I won't be able to get up again.'

Can panic attacks happen if you are not nervously exhausted?

The answer is yes, but there will always be some underlying anxiety either from the past or present as in this example.

The firm was sending me to America for six weeks. I felt delighted and made preparations for the trip. When I was in the travel agent's a few uneasy thoughts about the flight crept in. I wanted to talk to someone about it but felt a fool. When you are a 6'3" rugby-player it is quite hard to tell your friends you are anxious about flying.

I felt sure I would be all right when the time came and pushed it to the back of my mind. Two weeks before the flight I woke up in the middle of the night in a terrible state. I was scared stiff, my heart was racing and I felt confused. Convinced it was some terrible virus I called the doctor. He was kind and said he could see I was distressed but there was nothing physically wrong. He asked me to see him at the surgery the following day. His explanation of the panic attack was that the fear of the flight was nagging away in my

19

unconscious. He said he had a lot of patients who were panicky before trips. I was not convinced but took the two pills he offered me for each journey.

I had the same feeling but not so dramatic while I was in the luggage check-in queue, so he must have been right. I was glad to take one of his pills. The journey was fine; I did not need one on the return trip and I have not had a panic attack since. That was two years ago.

Obsessions

Obsessions are persistent thoughts or images which the sufferer feels powerless to dismiss even though he recognizes them as unpleasant, futile, or ridiculous.

Mild obsessions are common even in healthy people; a line of a song or part of an old conversation going around and around in the head, or a silly idea like; 'I will fail my exam unless I wear green and yellow striped socks.'

When these fixed ideas fill the mind and preoccupy the person so much that it disrupts his life, the condition is called obsessional neurosis, and professional help is needed. If the obsessions get to this stage then it is usually an indication that the sufferer has been under a nervous strain for some time.

Compulsions

When the anxiety caused by obsessive thoughts becomes severe, the sufferer changes his behaviour in an attempt to cope. This is called *compulsive behaviour*: actions, or avoidance of actions that don't make sense either to the sufferer or onlookers. The innocent childhood form of this could be avoiding stepping on lines in the pavement, or tapping the forehead three times before entering the classroom. It's quite common for children to develop these little rituals – perhaps it's their idea of an insurance policy against anxiety.

Common compulsive acts

These can include: continually checking – going back several times to make sure the gas has been turned off, or the door has been locked. The person knows he has turned it off, but as soon as he moves away his anxiety rises again and he feels the need to check again. Sometimes a pattern develops and his anxiety will subside if he checks a specific number of times. Life can be exhausting and frustrating when you have to make seven trips from the front door to the cooker before you can get out of the door, or five trips from the gate to the front door to check that it has been locked.

Hand washing, cleaning, counting or continually tidying are other common rituals. As the anxiety levels come down these distressing symptoms ease. Susan might say of her friend Penny, 'She has an obsession about germs; she is always cleaning her house.' Maybe Penny does spend a lot of time on what appears to be unnecessary housework, but if it is only part of a full life and she is happy and relaxed then it is unlikely to be obsessional. If, on the other hand, she thought about nothing *but* cleaning and germs and was unable to live a normal life, then this would be *obsessional neurosis*.

Phobias

We have seen that anxiety is a mix of emotions we feel when threatened. A phobia is an *intense* fear of a situation or object which would not normally worry other people (except, of course, those who suffered from the same phobia).

It is possible to develop a phobia about any situation or object in life, animate or inanimate. Phobias about situations where there could possibly be some danger, such as thunderstorms, heights or being faced with a snake, are often easier to understand; but the more bizarre ones like fear of feathers, buttons, or walking past a hole in the road, are often observed with scorn – 'Don't be stupid, how could anyone be so scared of buttons?'

It is important to realize that the terror experienced by the sufferer is the same whether his/her phobia concerns thunderstorms or encountering a woman in a green hat. Even the *thought* of the feared situation can cause a panic attack.

The most common phobias

Situations: Heights, enclosed spaces, the dark, being away from home.

Illness: Cancer, heart trouble, losing a limb.

Animals: Any animal, insect or bird (even ones never likely to be encountered) – a picture or mental image can provoke terror.

Social: Fear of meeting people either socially or in public, on buses, shopkeepers, hairdressers etc.

You might say we could all be afraid of some items in the above list; this is true, but it would not be a phobia unless our lives were completely disrupted by avoiding situations where the fear could be triggered – for example, being so afraid of dogs that you did not go out of the house at all.

Are you ill if you have a phobia?

If your phobia were spiders and someone placed one on your arm it would be a dreadful experience because of the chain reaction it would set up in your body, but this does not mean you are *ill*. You will learn later not only how to help your body after the event, but also how to prevent the phobia being triggered by physical causes, such as hunger.

Agoraphobia

Fear of going from the safety of the home is probably the most common phobic problem. It can range from a mild fear of going out – into shops or travelling etc. – to being completely housebound and severely anxious and depressed.

Treatment for phobias

Behaviour treatment, also known as desensitization or

exposure treatment, is usually very helpful. It involves regular and progressive exposure to the feared situation. The sufferer faces his fear in stages. In agoraphobia, for example, he would initially be encouraged to venture as far as the gate, then a few steps beyond the gate etc., or, if his phobia was cats, he would first be shown pictures of a cat and progress (supported by his therapist) to being able to touch a cat without fear. This treatment is very much more effective if the patient understands what is happening in his body (how one part of the nervous system is fast (the man in the red Ferrari), and the other part is slow (the man in the blue Morris Minor again) before he starts. It is also vital to teach him how to relax and control breathing.

It's no good just treating the mind   A report in *The Lancet*, 22 September 1984, supports this:

> Two groups of patients were treated for agoraphobia. One group had breathing re-training [page 91] and behaviour therapy; the other had only behaviour therapy. Both groups improved, but a six months' follow up of the first group showed further improvement, whilst the second group had slipped back to old behaviour.

This condition was formerly thought to be very difficult to treat. But with the increasing use of relaxation methods, and the realization that tranquillizers, far from being a help, were actually the cause of phobic symptoms in many patients (page 56) many more people are now being successfully treated. Some people do not need professional help. Self-help groups are very helpful, or a friend or relative can be your support.

Hyperactivity

In this state the person is so wound up with nervous energy that he is constantly on the move. The compulsion to move is overpowering. It can be productive when it is possible to harness it – working longer hours, for example – but it can also be aimless and associated with lack of concentration: 'I can't settle; one minute I am in the garden weeding, the next I am cleaning the bath and then I am rushing to take the dog out.'

Hyperactivity is not only difficult to endure, it is also difficult to live with. Energy caused by severe tension bursts out all over and the sufferer cannot relax. Muscles ache and they long for a rest but the body will not allow it. Rapid thoughts and compulsive talking accompany hyperactivity.

Lack of concentration

Even quite young people fear they are going senile because they cannot concentrate on reading, or even follow simple written instructions. They forget appointments, and become very worried about losing their memory. It is often more likely that because they are so tense, they have failed to take in the information rather than their memory letting them down. As the nerves recover the concentration comes back. Meanwhile, why not write yourself a few reminders: 'My concentration is poor because I am tense – what am I going to do about it?' Or 'Overbreathing causes lack of concentration.'

Insomnia

This is a particularly distressing symptom because you cannot escape from the worries of the day and you know you are going to feel worse the following day. If it is a long-term problem it can cause depression. Some people find it difficult to get off to sleep, others wake several times in the night or wake in the early hours of the morning. Disturbances include strange dreams, nightmares, panicky feelings, wind or the need to pass urine frequently.

Causes of insomnia

The many causes include: worry, excitement, pain, itching, lack of exercise and fresh air, breathing or digestive problems. A healthy bowel seems to play quite a large part in getting a good night's sleep. Perhaps this is because the bacteria in the bowel produce chemicals that make us sleepy.

What do I do about not sleeping?

This is going to be a disappointing section for people expecting some simple solution to this problem. Regrettably there isn't one. A disturbed night (unless it is for practical reasons like toothache or a crying baby) indicates that all is not well with your nerves and until you look after them you will not get a good night's rest.

Don't stay in bed

Preparation for sleep starts when you get up. It is a great mistake to sleep late habitually in order to catch up on lost sleep. This disturbs the normal body rhythm, you miss the brightest time of the day – (see further reading, page 112 and also pages 45–6) and end up feeling jetlagged all the time. Even if you just slump in front of breakfast television, make the effort to get up, have breakfast and keep to your routine.

Think about what you are doing

It is useless to rush around all day or even sit around in a tense state, then expect your body to gear down half an hour before you want to go to sleep. So often the cry is, 'I used to fall asleep the moment my head touched the pillow, what has happened?'

Get used to the idea that tired nerves are wayward nerves, and also that you must be working *against* your body in some way. If you feel you are not making progress and want to break your present sleeping pattern, you could ask your doctor to prescribe a sleeping pill for two or three nights (page 56).

The worst thing you can do is lie there worrying about not sleeping. Get up and move around. You could try some of the exercises in Part Two, particularly slow breathing (page 91). Massaging the soles of the feet and bathing them in very cool water can be soothing. The heart rate can be slowed down by gentle pressure on the eyeballs or have a snack and one of the night-time herbal teas, or a milky drink; you won't sleep if you are hungry. Some people find it helpful to listen to relaxation tapes in bed; a headset cuts out external noise and does not disturb your partner.

6

Causes of Exhausted Nerves

All the stresses of life

Magazines often list life problems according to their stress rating and ask you to add up your score – enough to invite a breakdown! It would have to be a very long list to include all the hurtful events in life, so if your problem is not here don't feel it is unimportant. Anything which worries or hurts you is a stress. No matter how many people tell you that it should not affect you, if it makes you unhappy, then it is on the list. *Adjusting to change is stressful.*

Death of a loved one
Death of someone you felt
  you should have loved
Divorce
Loss of a relationship
Physical illness
Disability
Loss of employment
Stress at work
Poverty
Retirement
Poor housing
Getting old
Growing up
Being born
Taking care of the elderly
Taking care of the young
Addictions
Spiritual problems

Taking care of the sick
Exams
Relatives moving away
Promotion
Getting married
Having a baby
Children leaving home
Learning difficulties
Going away from home
Going on holiday
Heavy physical work
Long hours
Poor working environment
Working to deadlines
Constant travel
Too much responsibility
  (particularly in the
  young)
The crying baby

Being unhappy about your appearance	Fear of being raped or mugged
Being worried about your sexuality	Even winning the football pools!

Because people feel guilty about being nervously ill, they often swoop on a list like this and say: 'Yes, I have this, this and this', as if they need to justify being nervously strained. If your nerves are in trouble then you have had pain either in the present or the past; it is as simple as that.

Sometimes it is better not to look too hard for what caused the problem. You may become aware of that as your nerves heal.

The past affects our nerves – stored pain

We start storing pain certainly from birth, and probably from our days in the womb. The infant comes into the world with the need to be fed, loved, protected and kept comfortable. If his needs are neglected and there is more pain (fear, anger, sadness etc.) than he can cope with then he tries to eliminate it by pushing it down with tension. This is the beginning of neurosis.

Frozen feelings – neurosis

It's time to defrost the freezer

The more a person has ignored his feelings, the more likely he is to have a 'drawer in the freezer of his unconscious', labelled, 'not very nice feelings – keep this drawer shut'. Fighting for space in there would be bulging packets, the use-by dates long expired, the labels reading feelings of rage, hate, jealousy, rejection, disappointment etc.

When does this cold storage start?

The foundation stone of the wall of neurosis is laid when pushing down the real feelings becomes the normal reaction. This can happen at any stage in life from early infancy. Neurosis is an illness of the feelings – a reaction to *pain*. The child who feels safe and loved and who is allowed to show his real feelings will not need to build a wall to hide behind. He can be himself and let others see who he is. But to endure the pain of the situation and make life bearable the unhappy child tightens his body to hold in his emotions (tension). He also manipulates his mind to alter his reaction to his unhappiness. This is the origin of *pretend*.

Pretend

Here is an example: The child in an institution who sits quietly rocking back and forth, does not cry and speaks politely when spoken to, is unlikely to be saying: 'I'm a quiet self-contained child contented with my lot.' He/she is really saying: 'I have tried screaming out in fear and rage because I am so unhappy. I still don't get what I need, so I switch off [become depressed]. Since I cannot get away from the misery I have to adapt to it.'

Should we still be doing this as adults?

We often continue to tighten our bodies (armouring) and manipulate our minds (depression) all our lives. Is it still appropriate to do this or is it time to get rid of pretend?

The behaviour of the hurt child

We have seen that the hurt child cannot behave normally, and either in order to cope, or please his parents, he freezes his real feelings and behaves neurotically. This is not a weak silly reaction, it is the *only* possible reaction for a child in pain. Clearly we are taught the habit of reacting to pain with anxiety or depression, and in order to break the habit we need to understand more about it.

The hurt child is still inside us

People who are in pain need love and understanding. The hurt child inside you is crying out for it. Whatever age you are it's not too late to start. How can you love anyone else if you don't nurture the sad/frightened child within? We are taught it is selfish to think of ourselves. To think *only* of ourselves is selfish, but learning to love the child within is an essential part of getting well.

Understanding the hurt child

Think of a little girl who is suffering from not being mothered in the way she needs. She is afraid, and thinks that if she is a very good girl and pleases her mother (remember her mother may love her but still not see her needs) life will be better. The girl loves her mother, so in devoting herself to pleasing her she is tricking her mind into believing she is happy playing the role of loving daughter. In reality, she is very angry and wants to say to her mother: 'Why do you only think of your own worries? I am frightened and miserable too – you are grown up, I am only little.'

Carrying the fear of losing love with us

She is likely to carry on with this charade as she grows up. She is afraid, although perhaps not consciously, of finally losing her mother's love. All the energy from the frustration and anger generated by the pretend reaction to her mother can leak out over the years in neurotic behaviour, which is often puzzling to her and onlookers, or it can also burst out in nervous exhaustion (breakdown) when she can't, or no longer needs to, hold in the anger.

Neurosis is a response to pain. It is sad that it is used as a term of abuse, or a put down. She/he is completely neurotic means she/he is silly, weak, does unpredictable things, cannot cope, is not very stable etc.

Children want to love those around them

Children not only want to be loved, but are very ready to love those around them. It is a great disappointment to them when they are treated as if their feelings don't matter. Being loved is not enough to give identity. You have to be acknowledged as a thinking, feeling human being. That is not to say you won't need guidance and discipline – you will, but if you are never able to express what you feel you wilt inside. How many 'dried up' people do you know?

Self-esteem

It is so common for a nervously ill person to say: 'I don't know who I am any more.' Is that surprising? We get into such a muddle, dodging our pain, trying to please others and occasionally ourselves (is the guilt worth it?) and relying on the opinion of others to tell us who we are.

Perhaps nervous illness is the unconscious saying: 'I have tried to guide you to better health but you are not listening. You are not a child now why don't you start to be yourself?'

7
Learning to Be Yourself
– Be Real

Our bodies want to be free from the armour of tension – they want to be real. Our minds want to be free too. Instead we do a juggling act with our feelings to suit those around us – bending this way or that for parents, teachers and then for spouse, children, boss, mother-in-law etc. When will it end? *Only when you love yourself enough to be real.*

This does not mean you have to stop loving the people who have played a part in your not being real, but that you owe it to yourself to acknowledge you are a unique, important person *whatever* your feelings are. It is your right to own them, they are yours. It is between you and God, or your conscience whether they are right or wrong.

No-one can tell you how you should think or feel. There is no *should* about feelings – feelings just *are*. When you stop fighting yours and start to accept them, life not only gets simpler, but also much more exciting. You may not be proud of how you feel about some things, but at least you are listening to whom you really are. Change is possible when you have accepted what you want to change from.

It is important to encourage those around you particularly young people, to own and express their feelings too.

Finding your own answers

You may have to accept that no-one is interested in your pain. There is nothing of medical significance wrong with you: you don't have a raised white cell count, an abnormal brain scan, or any interesting delusions which could cause a professional to say, 'Ah ha, just as I thought – classic'; it's just you, lonely in the middle of a family, struggling to keep going, one grey day after another, puzzled and guilty about how you feel; sitting in your mews flat, having had everything that money could buy, surrounded by dirty coffee cups and cigarette ends, stains on your skirt.

You have a choice

The following choices are available to you; only you can make them:

Are you willing to take responsibility for your physical and emotional health?

Are you willing to look at the part you are playing in your own unhappiness?

Are you willing to stop hurting yourself with alcohol, drugs, cigarettes, poor food, lack of exercise and fresh air?

Are you willing to stop feeling sorry for yourself ?

Are you willing to find out what your real needs are?

Are you willing to stop trying to please people all the time?

Can you accept that you can't change the people around you – you can only stop their attitude hurting you?

Can you accept that if you don't take care of yourself, you can be a terrible burden on those around you?

Can you accept you are causing a lot of your anxiety and depression by the way you think of yourself?

Are you willing to be *you*,.not what those around you think you should be?

Learning to be yourself – assertion

This can be very liberating and need not be accomplished by bulldozing through your relationships with anger saying: Look out, the real me is coming, I'm not going to be pushed around any longer. It can be done gently, and with love, but be prepared for criticism no matter how you tackle it.

33

Why are relationships such hard work?

Would relationships be such a strain if we accepted people the way they are and let them see us, warts and all? We have seen that real feelings produce healthy behaviour: a balanced outlook, ability to adjust to change, ability to cope. Suppressed feelings produce neurotic behaviour, anxiety and depression. As you start to be honest with yourself, being honest with those around you is the next step. Don't forget of course, that you cannot expect other people to change: you can only show them how *their* behaviour affects *you*.

Open honest communication

Imagine the following scene:

Place, the Dog and Duck: The venue for the weekly meeting of Bill, Tony and George. They have been friends for years. The time is early April. Each week they talk about sport, the office, and, according to the season, ground elder, aphids, their summer holiday, or the difference double glazing makes to the heating bills.

It's a bit early for ground elder and the greenfly are not yet in evidence; tonight they are going to talk about *feelings* (at least George is).

Bill and Tony are at the bar when George comes in. They exchange greetings then Bill notices George's eyes look red.

Bill	Hayfever already, old man?
George	(Rather sheepishly) No, actually, I've just had a few tears.
Bill and Tony	*Tears*! (They could not have been more embarrassed if George had just said he had wet himself).
Bill	(Gravely) Er, there's nothing wrong with Betty, is there George?
George	(Smiling) No, Betty's fine, everything's fine.

Tony   (His curiosity overcoming his embarrassment) Well what were you crying about.

George   I was not really crying. Life felt good; I was in the garden before I came out, the sun was still warm, a blackbird was picking moss from the gutter for its nest, and I could hear Betty playing a daft old song on the piano – I felt moved – tears came, so I let them. That's all it was. They told me that I had to let my feelings out when I had that little heart attack last year.

Bill and
  Tony   (Together after a stunned silence) Whose for a half then?

For the next hour they talk about the rust on Bill's car, the Common Market, and the new barmaid. George, looking happy and relaxed, makes his way to the loo. Tony and Bill's eyes meet over their beer glasses.

Bill   Do you think he is all right?

Tony   I don't know, but I do know he had a cousin in Carlisle who went a bit funny.

   Their lives are ruled by hiding their fears and sadness even from those close to them.

Bill is afraid of flying, of his wife dying before him, of being made redundant. He is sad about his father getting old and he still grieves for his dog. He keeps his feelings to himself.

Tony slept with the light on until he was married. His wife has no idea he is still very uneasy in the dark. She wishes he would be as organized about other things as he is about impending power cuts – boxes of candles and torches all over the place. He feels full of sadness and compassion about a neighbour's handicapped child, although he completely ignores the boy and avoids the parents if he can. He worries about his smoking but gets angry if it is mentioned. He loves his wife dearly, but rarely tells her so.

George has felt very guilty for years because he knew he had hurt his wife deeply by not wanting to see their stillborn son. He was gripped with a fear that he could not understand at the thought of seeing the dead baby. Some months after the birth he was dozing in front of the fire after a bout of 'flu and dreamt about a baby brother who had died at birth. George was four at the time. He felt distressed when he woke up and remembered how afraid he felt when he had been made to kiss the waxen little cheek. He also remembered being sent to an aunt and how she hurt when she scrubbed his face. The dream gave him some insight into his guilt, but he still could not bring himself to share it with his wife. When he did tell her years later (he had just come out of hospital) they both had a good cry and all his wife's hurt about George's apparent indifference to their loss disappeared.

What will others think?

If you do not show your real feelings to those around you, aren't you continuing with the mistakes started by the adults in your young life. When we are little we think: When I am grown up I will do this, this and this, but *do* we? Or do we just carry on hiding our feelings and playacting to make sure people won't dislike us, or worse still, walk away and leave us. We go on saying yes when we mean no, and no when we mean yes – *at what cost?*

8

Understanding the Nature
of Anxiety

*Understanding the nature of anxiety
can make it dissolve*

There are three main types of anxiety. What they all have in common are the physical symptoms. The causes may differ but the effect on the body is the same.

One young man wept during his first lesson on how to cope with anxiety. His tears were a mixture of relief and anger; years of pills could have been avoided if he had understood what was happening.

Types of anxiety

Outside anxiety

This is worry about real threats to the body or life circumstances, for example having an operation or losing a job. Sometimes the threat is so frightening the sufferer resists facing the source of his fear, and turns them into physical symptoms. He denies having any life problems and becomes evasive when the doctor asks if he has any worries. His denial is not an untruth; it is the truth as he sees it.

Inside anxiety

Here the fear comes from within and is caused by thoughts. Not thoughts like 'what will happen if I don't pass my exams' as in outside anxiety, but vague inner fears that the sufferer may only half recognize such as fear of losing control, of punishment, of being unlovable, of destructive feelings, perhaps towards family members. Sufferers often have an overwhelming fear of reprisal, for example, hating the boss, but not daring to show it. This can lead to self-hatred for what is seen as cowardice.

Judge and jury anxiety

The moral teaching we have as children is often another source of anxiety – worry about guilt. As we grow up, we continue to listen to the old records in our head and develop an internal judge and jury system far more severe than our original teachings. Here there is a muddle of anticipatory guilt: being terrified of doing anything which would be condemned by society, and a deep sense of frustration at having to go through the same stupid routines in order to keep our anxieties at bay. Here, for example, would be the man who always says 'Yes' because he can't stand the feelings of guilt when he says 'No'. He finds it very restricting to have to drive his mother fifteen miles to her friend's house to play bridge each Sunday, but would rather to do this than face the guilt.

Consider what disapproval means to you.

How do I feel when someone disapproves of me?

Anxious/hurt/trapped/depressed/like a naughty child?

Do I take actions to avoid disapproval, even over small things and then hate myself for being weak?

Do I do this over and over again?

The effects of the judge and jury system: what we do to our children. When we are constantly bombarded with: 'You must be a good child, consider the feelings of others', etc., what we are really hearing is: 'Beat yourself with sticks, turn yourself inside out, do whatever is necessary to achieve, appear socially acceptable, and *always* put the feelings of others first.' *There is something very wrong here.* Surely, we need to be taught to love others *as* ourselves and give our feelings equal consideration. A system that teaches us to ignore our own needs runs the risk of producing either self-effacing martyrs, or people who rebel, think only of themselves and take pleasure in riding roughshod over the feelings of others.

Guilt If the embryo judge and members of the jury are placed on their benches during childhood, the prisoner is on probation for ever and lives in fear of committing a 'crime' against society, because the thought of the punishment (guilt) is so distressing.

Some people are so worried about guilt they are permanently tense. Could this be the cause of many obsessions and phobias?

Freefloating anxiety

Where there is no obvious cause for the fear it is called freefloating – not attached to anything.

The perplexed person will say: 'I have absolutely nothing to be anxious about, yet I am in a state of fear all the time.' It is unlikely his subconscious would agree with him. It is more likely to be poking him to get rid of old fears, which he is trying to hold down with his intellect: 'I am financially secure, my wife loves me,' etc. This rationalizing does not work. You cannot dupe the subconscious – it has a record of the truth.

Ghosting: Robert's experience

Robert's way of coping with past pain was: 'If you don't think about it, it will go away.' That might work for a while but invariably a trigger from the present can bring the old feelings to life again and they nag away at you. This is called 'ghosting' – the unhooking of emotions of long ago from the unconscious. This is how it happened to Robert, although it does not need to be as dramatic as this. The next time you react to something with more anger or sadness than the situation deserves, ask yourself about the feelings. Is there more anger in you than you would like to admit? Is a sad thought enough to push you into depression because you hover on the edge of it all the time? Is there something from your past that you never really came to terms with?

Robert's only daughter was going off to work in France and he could not understand his reaction to this. He began to feel anxious and depressed and had a terrible sense of loss. It did not even make sense. He knew he would see her several times a year and, even more puzzling, he knew he was delighted she had the opportunity to go abroad.

Throwing out old feelings

After several talking sessions the feelings he had kept bottled up for years came pouring out.

Most of his childhood had been miserable. His mother left the family home when he was thirteen and he feared his father's temper so much that he had to work very hard to keep things running smoothly. This involved taking more than his share of responsibility for a younger sister. His father saw him as a sensible, caring boy. He did not see he was also full of anger and fear.

At first Robert was very embarrassed about crying over something that had happened so long ago, but saw how the old fear of loss had been affecting his present feelings. He was rather hard to live with as his anger surfaced but his family were supportive. He made good progress and said he felt physically lighter, as though a weight had been lifted off him. He had laid his 'ghost'.

9
Understanding the Nature
of Depression

Depression is very different from just being unhappy. When we are unhappy we can acknowledge the sadness about something in our lives, or in the lives of people close to us, but gradually the feeling affects us less and less, and we are able to be comforted and live normally in spite of a heavy heart.

In depression this is not so. The sufferer is unable to adjust to the painful feelings, so he switches them off and becomes emotionally dead. Unfortunately the good feelings which would balance his mood are also turned off, so it is difficult or impossible to comfort him.

It is sad that many people go through years of only being half alive not realizing they are suffering from a treatable illness. If your finger became numb and you could not use it you would be rushing off to the doctor to find the cause of the trouble. Why put up with numb *feelings*? Depression is often so sneaky; it creeps up on you, anaesthetizing your feelings little by little until your lack of emotions hardly registers and you accept your grey world as normal.

One young woman said:

Being depressed is like being in a room that needs decorating – you don't know it needs decorating so you can't do anything about it. All you know is a sense of dull misery and bewilderment that you have to stay in such a room.

When she realized she was suffering from depression, she said it was like being able to see the cracks on the wall. She felt the insight was optimistic, and she now knew why she had been in the grey room, but it also brought its problems: how

41

could she make it a better room to live in. It can be even more painful at first when the feelings start to wake up, and inevitably, anxieties rear their heads – how will I plaster the walls, will I ever find the right paint? etc.

But though scary it can also be very exciting because the good feelings are going to come through too. This is the start of recovery.

A young man described it like this:

It was as though I had undergone surgery and been under an anaesthetic for years – as I started to come out of the depression, my wound started to throb, but at least I was now awake enough to believe people when they were saying the throbbing would eventually go and I would be myself again.

What causes depression?

All the stresses of life – past and present (see Chapter 6).

Who is likely to suffer from depression?

Anyone and everyone can suffer from depression – although hereditary factors do come into some types of depression.

Terms used for depression (rightly or wrongly)

All the following mean roughly the same:

Mood disorder, affective disorder, reactive depression, endogenous depression, neurotic depression, manic depression, psychotic depression, retarded depression, agitated depression, personality disorder, dependent personality, masked depression, smiling depression.

Because this book deals with mild to moderate states of

anxiety and depression, psychotic depression will not be discussed. This is because it is part of a more severe illness which definitely needs professional help.

Types of depression

For our purposes it will be enough to look initially at three types of depression: outside depression, inside depression, and mixed depression.

Outside depression

This is sometimes called exogenous, reactive or neurotic depression. This is reacting to life circumstances with depression. When the change in the person's life is sad – for example, bereavement, divorce, loss of employment etc. – it is easy to see why there would be an alteration in mood. Sometimes, however, people can become depressed about very minor life changes which would not affect other people.

There can be many reasons for this. They can have a 'backlog' of events which have not been dealt with. They may have not had time to get over one blow, however small, before the next one landed, or they may habitually react with depression *because they were taught to react in this way*. In the same way that you can teach a child to be anxious, you can also teach it to be depressed.

Inside depression

This is also called endogenous or coming from within. Some professionals say this type of depression is caused by a fault in the body chemistry and the reason for this is unknown. But things do not go wrong in the body or mind without a reason. There may not be an obvious reason in the present life circumstances – 'What has he got to be depressed about, he loves his wife and family and drives a Porsche' – but there will certainly be a reason in the past.

Before you say: 'Ah, yes, but that was a long time ago and

he has had an easy time since then,' remember that if past hurtful feelings are not expressed they do not obligingly go away. They can leap out at you when you least expect it and force you to settle old scores. The pushed-down feelings which are most likely to cause depression later are anger, frustration, sadness, guilt, and of course the real killers – carrying around feelings of how unattractive or how worthless you are. It is vital to realize that the reality of the situation does not matter, it is the feelings that are important. For example, an unattractive man who has spent his life sweeping the road may never have experienced depression – he could feel very good about himself; whereas a man who looked like, say, Robert Redford, *and* had his bank balance, could be very depressed. No matter how successful you may be in the present, or how many people tell you what a wonderful person you are, if you are pushing around a wheelbarrow full of negative feelings about yourself, you are going to stay depressed. Tip those feelings onto the compost heap – express them – and you will recover.

Mixed depressions

Many people have a mixture of outside and inside depression – difficult life circumstances plus reduced ability to cope because of neurosis.

Agitated depression

Normally depression is associated with slowing down but in this type of depression the person is also very restless and anxious. He can't win – he can't even have the rest depression usually brings.

Smiling depression

Some people go to great lengths to hide being down; the joke-a-minute person who uses humour as a mechanism to hold in his pain and fool others. Perhaps it could be called the 'clown syndrome': smiling mouth and sad eyes.

Masked depression

Here the symptoms take a physical form – backache, headaches, digestive upsets, etc. The sufferer may not be aware of the cause of his trouble and deny he is depressed.

Manic depression

Self-help can only be recommended for the milder forms of this illness. It can, however, be used effectively with medical treatment. Taking care can help prevent recurrences. Manic depression is when the mood swings from very low to very high spirits. Some people with mania enjoy their 'highs', but many find them just as upsetting as the lows because they know their personality changes. It can be particularly distressing for relatives. The sufferer's thoughts and actions are so speeded up that he can work faster, be creative and generally achieve a great deal, but he can also be reckless about driving, spending money and making big decisions. He can have the same attitude to relationships – off with the old, on with the new. If you see a friend behaving untypically, suggest that his nerves are exhausted and encourage him to seek help. It may be quite a task; he may think life is great, but not for long. The nervous system cannot cope – what goes too far up has to come a long way down. The crunch will come.

Seasonal affective disorder (SAD)

SAD or winter blues is a recurrent depression which starts about the same time every year. When the amount of daylight diminishes in early autumn sufferers experience symptoms which grow worse as the days shorten.

It usually starts by increased need for sleep and losing concentration and progresses to depression, anxiety, irritability and loss of sexual interest. Other signs are aches and pains and cravings for sweet foods, bread, pastries, etc.

As spring approaches the symptoms improve and usually by about May sufferers recover and resume a normal life. For some, unfortunately, even though they feel better, the disruption caused by the illness year after year leads them into 'ordinary depression' because it becomes impossible to pick up the pieces of their lives each spring. Studies are interrupted, jobs lost and relationships ruined.

Happily, once the nature of the depression is recognized the illness can be avoided. It is not a new condition but a newly discovered one. Recent research is very exciting. The cure is to be out more in daylight, or for severe sufferers to be exposed to special lights (full spectrum lighting). The pineal gland is stimulated by light and this keeps the hormones balanced and prevents the problem.

For mild symptoms spending 20 to 30 minutes outdoors (without dark glasses) in the brightest part of the day and perhaps working near a window may be enough. If the symptoms are severe the installation of full spectrum lighting in the home may be necessary. Some psychiatric departments now treat SAD sufferers with light therapy, which involves daily exposure to high intensity light which is similar to sunlight (see further reading, page 112).

What does depression feel like?

Here are some descriptive comments made by sufferers:

I have no interest in anything or anyone; I know I still love my family but I can't *feel* it.

I feel exhausted; my thoughts are slow and even talking is an effort. I struggle to get the kids out to school then just sit at the breakfast table and stare at the wall until lunch time.

I feel so worthless and guilty.

Time seems to stand still.

There seems to be a grey mist over everything – I just want to stay in bed and pull the blanket over my head.

I can't bear to watch television in case I see something sad – I can't stop crying.

It's such an effort to be with people – nobody understands – I have to pretend to be normal; it's agony.

All the things I did cheerfully now seem like impossible tasks – even making a meal or putting the milk bottles out.

I used to love clothes and make-up; some days I don't even wash or dress.

I look at people and feel bewildered by their interest in things; reading, playing golf, painting the house – I think, why do they bother. Everything seems pointless.

I feel such a burden to my family; would they be better off without me?

If only I could sleep; I wake between four and five every morning.

If only I could get off to sleep; it is often three o'clock before I drop off and then I can't rouse myself in the morning.

If only I could cry; the tears are inside but I can't get them out.

I worry all the time about the future; it looks so bleak.

Have I been so bad? Is this a punishment?

I feel as if there is a weight in my stomach.

My chest feels heavy; I keep sighing.

I keep thinking I have heart trouble or cancer; I can't stop talking about it.

I will do anything to avoid sex.

I seem to get a little better as the day wears on and then I stay up late because I dread the mornings. *Or:*

I can struggle through the day but the feeling gets worse towards evening.

Be encouraged by the feelings of others. You are not alone, you are not going round the bend and you *will* recover. Other people do; why not you?

Glimpses of getting better

It can be slow at first. Here are some comments:

I looked at Ben in his cot and for a few seconds I could actually feel my love for him; it was such a relief. I know my feelings will come back now.

I woke up and thought I'll have some coffee and go out for a paper; I had not thought about a paper for months. I usually think, 'Oh God, how will I get through the day.' It did not last, but it gave me hope.

I was always ready with a negative answer when someone tried to encourage me.

I had to force myself to go to Polly's school play and was surprised how well I coped.

My wife was angry; I went into the garage to escape. When I went indoors I was amazed; two hours has passed. I had tidied the tools and potted some bulbs. Apart from pushing myself to work it was the first time I had got out of the chair for weeks.

It was the first time for years that I had not died inside when Nick mentioned a holiday.

Food has begun to taste again and I actually bought a magazine the other day.

I don't argue with Mary so much. I am shocked at how selfish I have been; so wrapped up in myself I did not give her a thought.

It took me a long time to accept it was depression but when I did I started to go forward.

I feel as if a curtain has been lifted. I am having more and more good days, although when I am having a bad day it's hard to remember the good ones.

It was a small thing but I still remember it. The colour of the grass registered. It was a lovely green and I could *see* it. It was like coming out of prison.

10

What is a Nervous Breakdown?

This generally means having anxiety and/or depression to a degree where a normal life is not possible.

Psychiatrists spend a lot of time discussing the difference between anxiety and depression. It must be difficult for the general practitioner to make the distinction in a six-minute consultation. Sometimes it is clearly more one than the other, but very often the nervously exhausted person is suffering from a mixture of the two. It can happen that as the anxiety feelings ease the depression starts, or vice versa.

The common and much-feared term nervous breakdown mistakenly conjures up an image of someone being transported to a psychiatric department in a straightjacket. Claire Weekes, in her books, very wisely uses the words 'sensitized nerves' instead of nervous breakdown. Before using other terms perhaps this 'bogeyman' could be laid to rest once and for all; these are only words. If someone is told they are having a breakdown they are understandably afraid. If they are told their nerves are exhausted or oversensitized, it means the same thing, but it does not alarm them so much. We all have nervous breakdowns regularly – it's only a matter of degree. If our nervous systems cannot cope with repeated stresses, reactions like 'blowing your top' or 'losing your cool' result. These could be seen as mini-breakdowns. If the nervous system does not 'hold up' then it must break down! A major breakdown can be said to be a major reaction to a major degree of stress (pain).

Do people recover from nervous breakdowns?

Of course, broken down nervous systems can be built up again. Some years ago MIND, The National Association for

49

Mental Health, produced a poster showing a healthy, pretty young girl saying: 'I have forgotten my nervous breakdown, but my friends haven't.' What it expresses is a sad reflection on our attitude to nervous illness. It is easy to forget a person's gallbladder operation or broken hip, but a nervous breakdown is rather a different matter. The memory of the changed behaviour – mood swings, irritability, suspiciousness – often lingers, and doubts about whether this is the normal personality remain: 'Will it happen again?' Happily, the person who has recovered from a breakdown is often more stable than those who are ignoring the state of their nerves.

A breakdown can have the effect of a giant springcleaning of the unconscious – the floodgates are open, the person has lost his armour and is too weak to hold back his pain any longer. The tremendous energy involved in the long-term suppression of feelings is discharged, leaving the person tired, but in a state where it is possible to heal.

Treatments for nervous breakdowns

Man has always looked for a substance to help him cope with fear. He has found many that temporarily relieve his symptoms – but at what cost? A deterioration in in his physical health (you cannot swallow poisons daily and expect to keep healthy), and the inevitable change in personality that comes from long-term sedation or stimulation of the nervous system. There is also the problem of dependence.

At the moment self-help groups and the statutory services all over the country (and abroad) are endeavouring to clean up a 20-year mess caused by the use of tranquillizers and sleeping pills known as the benzodiazepines (see Chapter 11, page 56).

Going to the doctor with nerves

Many patients reveal only a few of their symptoms to the

doctor. They are too embarrassed to recount what seems to be a long list of unrelated problems, and often hesitate to ask questions.

An ideal consultation

The sick person needs to understand what is making him ill:

Your tests are negative, you don't need drugs or surgery, but you do need help. Because you have had so much stress your body is producing too much adrenalin and that is the cause of those strange feelings. You are going to have to learn to slow down. There is a class here on Tuesdays at 7.30 pm.

If you feel desperate for a rest, I could give you tranquillizers for up to two weeks, but it would be better if you could manage without them. It's not safe to give these drugs for long periods, you could become addicted to them and they can cause depression. The other problem with them is that you cannot adjust to your problems if you suppress them with sedatives. It's like splinting an injured arm; useful for a short time, but the arm will not regain full strength until the splint is removed.

I'll tell the counsellor you are coming to the class and can you come back if you don't feel you are making progress?

After this consultation the patient leaves feeling that his misery has been acknowledged, and he has had some explanation, however brief, about the cause of his symptoms. He knows there will be ongoing support.

Unfortunately, it is not an ideal world and few doctors have access to a counsellor or relaxation therapist. Happily there are doctors who are moving away from the prescription pad and realize the value of education and support. Many arrange longer consultations and provide their patients with written information on anxiety and depression.

An unsatisfactory consultation

What the doctor may see as an optimistic, reassuring consultation – 'All your tests are negative; it's all nerves, just go home and forget about it' – usually leaves the patient miserable and confused. The symptoms are still there and he has no idea how to get rid of them. He may have longed for a test to reveal the cause of his misery. What he needs to know is that there is a cause, although it may not be the hoped-for low thyroid levels, anaemia or hernia that could be cured with a magic pill or surgery.

He leaves the surgery knowing he should feel relieved about the tests but finds it hard to accept that so many symptoms can be caused by nerves. Is it his fault? If there is no reason for the symptoms and no treatment then he must be imagining he is feeling so awful. He may already be aware of the reactions of those around him to people with 'nerves', and may fabricate a story rather than face the humiliation of telling family and friends.

The doctor has nerves too

While there is no excuse for a doctor being indifferent to your emotional pain, handing out lethal pharmacological cocktails, or for abruptly stopping your tranquillizers, if you consider what his life involves, it might dissipate some of your anger towards him. How many times have you shouted at someone: 'I can't do everything'? When you think of it that is just what a doctor is expected to do. Everything from the needlework necessary for minor surgery – to diagnosis of every known disease. He also has to cope with some very difficult situations, for instance how to get through a consultation with a violent patient, or take the anger of grieving relatives. Don't forget he is a human being too, and has only the limits of his own personality in which to work. He could be anxious and depressed too. There was a report a few years ago suggesting that the higher the doctor's anxiety levels were the more likely he was to prescribe tranquillizers for his patients.

Doctors are often not very good at accessing the emotional states of their patients: this may be because not enough time is given to this during their training, or it may be due to their own embarrassment or fear. They are not robots trained to label disease and excise cysts. Having to deal with the emotions of others must at times be like rubbing salt into their own wounds. A white coat does not make them immune. Imagine what it must be like to have three recently bereaved people in one surgery when your own wife is terminally ill – who supports the doctor? It is a pity the fear of being non-professional does not allow doctors to share what they are feeling. Our hurts are a great leveller, the one thing we all have in common.

Why is nervous illness so misunderstood?

Because there is nothing dramatic to be seen, the sufferer is often treated like a hypochrondriac or malingerer. It is easy to understand a fever in someone with pneumonia, or why there is pain in a broken limb, but much harder to accept that nervously ill people have disabling symptoms too. If the person who is obviously physically ill or injured becomes irritable or depressed, this is seen as part of the illness and treated with concern. But people with nervous troubles often get little sympathy unless they become seriously ill and need inpatient care.

How do we know when our nerves are in danger?

The early warnings sent out by the nervous system are quite vague and often ignored. They include: losing energy, feeling irritable, a change in eating or sleeping habits and generally losing interest in life. If you don't slow down the nervous system gives up and lets chaos reign – hence all the symptoms.

The person who says: 'This came on suddenly, I was fine last week,' has really not noticed how strained his nerves have become. They are now forcing him to stop and take notice. How useful it would be if, from our infancy, every time we pushed our nerves too far we came out in a crop of black spots. We would then be aware of the damage we were doing and could slow down until the spots disappeared.

11

Drug and Non-Drug Treatments
for Depression and Anxiety

Drug treatment for anxiety

When tranquillizers and sleeping pills – Valium (diazepam),
Librium (chlordiazepoxide), Ativan (lorazepam), Mogadon
(nitrazepam) etc. – were first used over 20 years ago, they
were hailed as wonder drugs, the pill for all ills. Whatever was
wrong with you just take a Valium and it would go away. It
was said then that they were non-addictive and that the side-
effects were minimal. Unfortunately, it is now known that the
opposite is true, and millions of people are suffering through
the long-term use of these drugs.

Tranquillizers – there is no need to panic

If you are taking the drugs mentioned below please note:

(1) You may not be dependent on them.
(2) If you are dependent, by a careful reduction plan and
    looking after yourself, you can make a full recovery.
(3) How do you know if you are dependent? If you feel the
    pills are no longer working the way they did, and you
    have to increase the dose to get the same effect, or if
    you feel ill when you stop taking them then you could
    be dependent.
(4) Consult your doctor and read *Coming off Tranquilliz-*
    ers and Sleeping Pills (see further reading, page 112) it is
    a complete guide to withdrawal.

Doctors are much more informed about withdrawal than they
were, but in case you need information for your doctor here
are the latest guidelines for professionals.

Guidelines

From: *Current Problems* (Committee on Safety of Medicines), Number 21, January 1988

Benzodiazepines, Dependence and Withdrawal Symptoms

There has been concern for many years regarding benzodiazepine dependence (*British Medical Journal* 1980, 910–912). Such dependence is becoming increasingly worrying.

Withdrawal symptoms include anxiety, tremor, confusion, insomnia, perception disorders, fits, depression, gastrointestinal and other somatic symptoms. These may sometimes be difficult to distinguish from the symptoms of the original illness.

It is important to note that withdrawal symptoms can occur with benzodiazepines following therapeutic doses given for short periods of time.

Withdrawal effects usually appear shortly after stopping a benzodiazepine with a short half-life. Symptoms may continue for weeks or months. No epidemiological evidence is available to suggest that one benzodiazepine is more responsible for the development of dependency or withdrawal symptoms than another. The Committee on Safety of Medicines recommends that the use of benzodiazepines should be limited in the following ways.

Uses

As Anxiolytics
  (1) Benzodiazepines are indicated for the short-term relief (two to four weeks only) of anxiety that is severe, disabling or subjecting the individual to unacceptable distress, occurring alone or in association with insomnia or short-term psychosomatic organic or psychotic illness.
  (2) The use of benzodiazepines to treat short-term 'mild' anxiety is inappropriate and unsuitable.

As hypnotics [sleep-inducing drugs]
  (3) Benzodiazepines should be used to treat insomnia only when it is severe, disabling, or subjecting the individual to extreme distress.

Dose

(1) The lowest dose which can control the symptoms should be used. It should not be continued beyond four weeks.
(2) Long-term chronic use is not recommended.
(3) Treatment should always be tapered off gradually.
(4) Patients who have taken benzodiazepines for a long time may require a longer period during which doses are reduced.
(5) When a benzodiazepine is used as a hypnotic, treatment should, if possible, be intermittent.

Precautions

(1) Benzodiazepines should not be used alone to treat depression or anxiety associated with depression. Suicide may be precipitated in such patients.
(2) They should not be used for phobic or obsessional states.
(3) They should not be used for the treatment of chronic psychosis.
(4) In case of loss or bereavement, psychological adjustment may be inhibited by benzodiazepines.
(5) Disinhibiting effects may be manifested in various ways. Suicide may be precipitated in patients who are depressed, and aggressive behaviour towards self and others may be precipitated. Extreme caution should therefore be used in prescribing benzodiazepines in patients with personality disorders.

Drug treatment for depression

If you are severely depressed you must see your doctor. He will probably prescribe antidepressant drugs. These can be very effective for some people and dramatically improve the quality of their lives. It is unwise, however, to use them for mild or moderate depression – not only because a great many people recover completely from depression without any treatment at all, but also because these drugs can bring problems, including side-effects of weight gain, headaches, confusion, panic, dry mouth, and constipation.

Dos and dont's

The drugs commonly used are the tricyclic antidepressants. The MAOIs (monoamine-oxidase inhibitor) antidepressants are also used but less often because of their side-effects and dangerous interaction with certain foods. Lithium and drugs called phenothiazines are used to sedate in mania.

(1) Beware of repeat prescriptions. See your doctor if you: develop a rash, or experience severe side-effects; or if you have been on them a while and start to feel 'high'.

(2) When it is time to withdraw, do it *gradually*. *This is very important.* There is no doubt that people coming off antidepressants may experience withdrawal symptoms, very similar to the symptoms of tranquillizer withdrawal. They do go, in time, so be patient and try not to rush back for more drugs.

(3) Don't expect the pills to sort out your emotional problems – that's *your* job.

(4) Don't think you can swallow pills and not adjust your lifestyle – that won't work either.

Non-drug treatment for anxiety and depression – talking therapies

Hand-holding approach – counselling

This can be *non-directive*, where you can talk in a warm friendly atmosphere and use the counsellor as a sounding board for your thoughts, and in doing so work out your own answers; or it can be *directive* where you are taught how to work through the situation.

The archaeological dig approach – exploration

The aim of this therapy is to increase insight, and uncover past pain. When 'corpsed-hurts' are faced and given a decent burial they become less hurtful. The patient is encouraged to see that emotional problems of the present are linked to past feelings. New insight often helps people to get off the roundabout of continually making the same mistakes. An example of this would be an adult who gains insight into why she rushes from one disastrous relationship to the next – she cannot bear to be alone; she is trying to avoid the feelings of fear and abandonment of her childhood.

The open window approach – ventilation

Getting something off your chest can be voicing it angrily; 'blowing off steam', or the very dramatic outpouring of emotion with sobbing or rage known as *catharsis*.

Abreaction ('living through') is the removal of the pain of a forgotten experience by uncovering it and reliving it. For example, one young woman relived the experience of sexual abuse which she had suffered as a child. She did not make much progress with counselling but was finally able to face her childhood fear and humiliation when she joined a group of adults at the rape crisis centre. She felt safe with people who had suffered the same experience.

Abreaction is usually very helpful except for people who are severely mentally ill.

Light treatment

In the past few years some very exciting work has been done on the effect of full spectrum lighting on some depressions, particularly SAD (seasonal affective disorder), winter depression (see page 45, and further reading, page 112).

12
Physical Reasons for Anxiety and Depression

Physical causes of nervous feelings

These include: hormonal changes (puberty, premenstrual tension (PMT), the menopause, hysterectomy, childbirth), certain glandular disorders such as thyroid problems, anaemia, infections, chronic physical pain.

It may be chicken and egg situation with some of these conditions; tired nerves causing bodily dysfunction, which in turn causes anxiety and depression.

Body–mind interaction

It is agreed that the body affects the mind and mind affects the body; but if someone is anxious or depressed, there is often a tendency to concentrate on looking for psychological causes and, as a result, physical causes can be overlooked. Even if the condition has been caused by stress, there are many instances where psychological help alone does not work, and unless the physical symptoms are also treated, the patient does not make progress.

Allergies: Conditions often mistaken for 'nerves'

The word allergy has been around since the beginning of the century. It describes an altered reaction in the body tissue to a substance which is not normally poisonous. This is an allergic reaction.

The contact can be from eating, drinking, touching or inhalation.

No-one is surprised by familiar allergic reactions like

hayfever, asthma, or even a severe reaction to some foods. What is more difficult to accept is that many people have chronic food or chemical allergies which produce multitudinous symptoms, including anxiety and depression. It is important these are recognized as symptoms coming from altered brain chemistry (caused by allergens) and *not* neurosis. All the psychological tricks in the book will not work if the cause of the change in mood is due to an allergy to wheat (or to anything else).

Yeast infections (Thrush – Chronic Candidiasis)

It has been acknowledged for the past ten years that many drugs (antibiotics, steroids, the birth pill, and more recently tranquillizers and sleeping pills) weaken the immune system and allow organisms normally present in the body to multiply rapidly. The fungus *Candida albicans* is one of them. It crowds out the good bacteria in the bowel and plays havoc with the digestive system. It produces numerous chemicals including female hormones. This is probably one of the reasons for the mood swings and severe premenstrual tension experienced by so many people who have this problem.

Because chronic candidiasis produces so many symptoms, including anxiety and depression, it is often diagnosed as a psychosomatic (mind affecting the body) illness, and people who have been incorrectly diagnosed have spent years going back and forth to psychiatric outpatient departments. The treatment they receive – more and more pills – makes matters worse and many people have turned to alternative medicine for help. The body will often tell us what is wrong if we choose to 'listen' to it. So many candida sufferers have said, 'I knew something in my body was affecting my head.'

Treatment is effective although it can take several months, and consists of antifungal agents (not always drugs), diet and supplements, including vitamins and minerals. Live yogurt cleans up the digestive tract and discourages the growth of the candida.

Although the candida problem is growing to enormous proportions, in general the medical world has been slow in recognizing what is happening. They tend to think that thrush (candida) only flourishes in the vagina or in babies' mouths.

Endless investigations

Patients with candida (and/or allergies) often have full gastrointestinal investigations (tubes poked into every possible place) and the results are invariably negative. The diagnosis is usually, 'the irritable bowel syndrome'; this really means: 'I cannot find a cause for your symptoms'. The high fibre diet usually recommended *always* makes the symptoms worse. This is not surprising since it would include foods that 'feed' the yeast. There are several helpful books around which describe the anti-candida diet fully. A good choice would be *Candida Albicans: Is Yeast Your Problem?* (see further reading, page 112).

Candida symptoms commonly reported

Abdominal Discomfort, bloating, gas, wakefulness, constipation/diarrhoea, frequent cystitis which does not respond to antibiotics, vaginal discharge, infection in the penis with soreness and discharge, mouth infections, ear infections (often a watery discharge which makes the skin around the ear sore), depression, anxiety.

Other problems are nail bed infections, athlete's foot, scalp problems (Selsun shampoo is effective), sores in the nose, cracks at the side of the mouth, coated sore tongue and inside of cheeks. The soft palate and throat can also be affected. In fact some people say they feel inflamed from the mouth to the anus (which also becomes sore and itches).

Urinary Candida could be the cause of the endless 'cystitis' seen in some nervous people. Cultures of their urine fail to produce organisms and symptoms do not respond to antibiotics. Sugary and yeasty foods, and alcohol make the symptoms worse. Always see your doctor if you have persistent abdominal or urinary symptoms. If he can find nothing wrong (there is no reliable test for candida, and he is probably unlikely to think of investigating for this anyway) you might want to seek a doctor specializing in clinical nutrition. Unfortunately this is rarely available under the National Health Service so if money is a problem you can use self-help methods: the health of many people has dramatically improved after following the instructions in the candida books (see further reading, page 112).

Fungal skin problems   Fungal skin problems are sometimes mistaken for nervous rashes. These can appear as dry, scaly red patches appearing anywhere on the body, but more usually over the cheek bones, at the sides of the nose, by the ears and on the hands.

Food and chemical sensitivities   Because the immune system is weakened, food and chemical allergies and candida often go together. Common complaints are: palpitations, flushing, headaches, light-headedness, abdominal bloating or breathlessness after eating certain foods or being near petrol fumes, gas fires etc. There are lots of useful books around on this subject to help discover which foods are causing your problems by using elimination diets; they also suggest how to rid your home of unnecessary chemicals. If your symptoms are severe it would be wise to seek professional help. Your doctor would be able to arrange allergy testing for breathing problems or hayfever, but it would be unlikely for him to be able to refer you for food allergy testing.

Myalgic encephalomyelitis (ME) or malingerer's disease

Also known as Royal Free disease, this is a chronic illness

which produces bouts of extreme tiredness in the muscles and brain. It can start with an illness like glandular fever or 'flu; sometimes it is so severe people have to give up work for a time. For decades, sufferers from this condition have been classed as malingerers or hypochondriacs. ME was first recorded about 50 years ago, but only in the past few years has there been a sharing of information amongst sufferers and doctors. ME is often mistaken for nervous illness because the symptoms include anxiety, depression and lethargy; it is also sometimes called the 'yuppie disease'. The immune system is also affected and multiple allergies and candida can be present.

Research is being carried out at St Mary's Hospital London and elsewhere, but as yet there is no answer in conventional medicine. Complementary medicine has helped many people to recover completely. The important aspects of treatment are: *rest*, a healthy diet, fresh air, daylight, keeping the bowel as clean as possible by preventing constipation, and restoring the normal balance to the gut bacteria. Any therapy which promotes relaxation and natural healing is also recommended. Tranquillizers and antidepressants rarely help this condition; they merely add more poisons to a body already struggling hard to excrete the poisons caused by the virus (see further reading, page 112).

Chronic pain as a cause of nervous exhaustion

It is not only the discomfort of pain that affects the nerves, but also the continual tension in the muscles. The person with even mild chronic pain never completely relaxes. Remember the fireman: when he tenses his muscles and increases his breathing rate his adrenalin levels go up. It needs to be repeated over and over again that when this happens, whatever the cause, anxiety, irritability and other nervous symptoms can result. People in pain often overbreathe in an attempt to control the pain. How this affects anxiety levels is discussed in Chapter 16.

Nutritional deficiencies as a cause of anxiety and depression

When the nerves are under stress, there is an enormous increase in the need for some vitamins and minerals. Poor appetite and faulty absorption often result in severe depletion. Even if you are a comfort eater and quite weighty, you can still be lacking in minerals and vitamins.

Common signs of vitamin deficiencies

(1) A tongue which is: swollen/sore/smooth/shiny red, sore and bright red at the tip, swollen taste buds, patches like a map, deeply fissured, swollen veins under the tongue.

(2) Bleeding gums, mouth ulcers, gum boils, cracks at the corners of the mouth, peeling lips, recurrent herpes.

(3) Slow healing of wounds, altered taste sensation, bruising easily, falling hair.

(4) Cramp and tired muscles.

These symptoms usually respond quickly to the correct supplements. Consult your doctor to see if he can guide you, or read one of the many books on the subject, such as the excellent *Nutritional Medicine* (see further reading, page 112).

It is important to follow guidelines because you could create more problems if you don't. For example: long-term continuous use of vitamin B_6 can cause neurological problems; large doses of vitamin D are toxic; and vitamin B complex can be a strong stimulant – fine if you are depressed but not if you are anxious and sleepless. Some vitamin B complexes (often ones containing yeast) can also cause cystitis, abdominal bloating, skin rashes and itching around the anus.

Nervous symptoms often take a physical form. We have seen that certain bodily functions are particular targets for anxiety and depression. In some people the fear, anger and sadness they experience comes out in physical symptoms. This is called somatizing. There is often an unhappy memory which causes symptoms to be 'laid down' in a particular place. The event is often recalled when tension is released, say in a shoulder, during physical therapy such as massage. The astonished patient comes in with a sore shoulder, which he sees as entirely physical, and ends up crying about a sad or frightening incident which happened in the distant past. Take away the tension, and the emotional pain can be released.

Here are some examples of how releasing emotional pain can help alleviate physical pain.

One young man came for help with a pain in his right knee, although it was clear he was also a little depressed. The pain (and depression) had come and gone for years. He had not mentioned the depression to his doctor, in fact, he did not realize the feeling *was* depression. He had his knee examined several times, but the cause of the pain remained a mystery.

During his therapy he remembered being slapped continually by his mother as he sat by her in the car. When he jumped about or argued with his brother, his right knee took the punishment. After he recalled this he became very angry and said, 'She is not going to slap me down this time.' After he had announced his engagement his mother had become cold and distant. It was then that his symptoms returned. His emotional progress was slow although his knee improved rapidly. At first he felt a lot of anxiety when he started to express his feelings – he felt he was hurting his mother. Who had been hurting him for years? She gave him a lot of love and approval, yes, but only if he lived his life in accordance with her wishes. He was a gentle person and the thought of open, honest communication (see Chapter 7) worried him. He was finally convinced that it could be done with love, and indeed had to be done, if he wanted to be well and live his own life.

One young woman had a cancer phobia: her mother had died from cancer of the bowel when she was 29. The woman

66

was approaching this age, and was convinced that the same fate awaited her. For several years she had complained of abdominal pain, and was jumping on and off the scale about seven times a day to see if she had lost weight. The negative result of numerous tests still could not convince her she had no organic disease. By sharing her feelings with others she could eventually see that tension was causing her abdominal discomfort and she lost all her symptoms. She gained 4½ kg in weight and started playing squash.

These are only illustrations of how emotional pain can be released. It is not always necessary to have a therapist or join a group. Loosening up your body with swimming or yoga can have the same effect (see Part Two).

13

Misdiagnosis

This can be very hurtful for the patient. Negative remarks can eat away at self-esteem and fill him/her with self-doubt. Have any of these unhelpful comments ever been directed at you:

Pull yourself together.
You are just anxious.
You are just depressed.
You enjoy the attention of being ill.
This pain is hysterical.
This is all in your head.

Incidentally, the next time anyone tells you to 'pull yourself together', smile and say, 'I would really like to do that. Can you tell me how I can do it?' It is unlikely that they would have any valid answers for you. Of course there are those who malinger, but for those who don't, people with nervous troubles longing to be well, it seems very unjust to keep pointing the finger at them. They have a double burden to endure: their distressing symptoms and the degradation of being told: 'You enjoy ill health.' There seems to be little to enjoy in having so much sick leave that you lose your job, are never without discomfort, and are a constant source of anxiety to those around you.

Take the following example: Ruth, a 30-year-old computer programmer had complained of abdominal pain on and off for four years. She felt the doctor was dismissing her because she had shown a history of nervous troubles in her early 20s.

The nagging pain dragged her down as did the 'are you here again' look during her regular visits to the surgery. She tried every doctor in the practice. One prescribed antidepressants. These gave her headaches, she gained 6 kg (a stone) in weight, and the premenstrual tension she had always suffered became unbearable. She continued to complain of abdominal pain and was eventually sent to a consultant. Investigative surgery revealed she had a notoriously painful gynaecological (womb) condition.

Years later she cried bitterly during a counselling session saying that not one person had said 'sorry you were right', or 'that was bad luck'.

People who do invent their symptoms

It cannot be denied that this does happen, and it is a source of irritation to those around, but surely, in many instances, the person who exaggerates, or invents physical pain needs as much attention as the person with an obvious physical problem. He is like a child who says his leg hurts, when in reality he has a very sore throat – he cannot localize his pain. He knows he is hurting, but he is not sure where.

Invented pain is usually treated as a moral issue – someone trying to deceive. It may be deception, but not at a conscious level. If people are not hurting, then there is no pain, and they simply get on with their lives. Perhaps we have grown up with the idea that physical pain is the only allowable pain. So many people say they have no trouble cancelling an engagement if they have a cold or sore throat, but feel anxiety and guilt if they have to change arrangements because they are too depressed to function. They often invent something physical and then worry about the lie, or feel degraded because they have had 'flu' once again.

The boy who goes to his father showing him a bloodied knee is likely to have the injury washed and covered with a sticking plaster. What would happen if he went to him and said he was afraid or sad: 'Afraid? Big boys of seven aren't afraid,' or 'What have you got to be sad about? We are off on holiday next week.' Emotional pain? All a bit embarrassing really – not very British. Is it any wonder the psychiatric departments are full?

PART TWO

Self-help Therapy for Anxiety and Depression

14

Being Your Own Therapist

You may feel you do not need outside help and want to see how much progress you can make on your own. The results can often be dramatic when people start to love themselves, give up pretending, and really learn how to relax.

Catharsis and abreaction (see Chapter 11) can happen spontaneously when you are not having treatment. It can be a little alarming if you don't know what is happening, but it should be welcomed. You will feel better as a result of it. The example of Paula, below, illustrates this trigger effect.

Paula's marriage was happy and she enjoyed her part-time work. She had suffered periods of depression all her life, although they were not disabling enough for her to seek help; she could still function. She came for help when she was confused and depressed after her mother died.

She felt she was grieving normally for her, but was surprised by her mounting feelings of hate for her father. He had been dead for some years and she thought she had forgotten about how miserable he made her young life. She started to dream about him and wake up feeling depressed. He filled her waking thoughts for days and she could not even escape from him in sleep.

She was feeling particularly strung-up with premenstrual tension one day coming home from work. The sound of piano-playing came through an open window. The memory it brought back made her feel sick with rage: she was nine years old, and being shaken violently by her father; he was angry because she was reluctant to practise the piano. Her timid mother always urged her to keep quiet and not upset her father.

After a few days of being restless and tearful everything poured out. Her astonished husband came home to find her shouting abuse at her father for his cruelty, and to her mother, for not protecting her. She was tearing up an old box of music.

After the 'confetti' had stopped flying, she dissolved into tears, and said she felt a great sense of release; she now no longer needed to keep quiet about her misery. She could get rid of it. Although she knew her actions seemed childish she continued because of the great sense of satisfaction they brought. Discharging so much pent-up emotion left her drained, but feeling that she was true to herself for the first time in her life.

Cognitive therapy – the 'change your thinking approach'

This treatment helps to overcome restrictions in everyday life by breaking the vicious circle of negative thoughts. Fear-provoking thoughts are changed by repeatedly replacing them with positive encouragement.

Self-talk

This is just what the name implies. By repeating instructions to ourselves either aloud or quietly we can break negative thinking habits. If you were learning to play a new piece on the piano and stumbled repeatedly at the same phrase, practising over and over again would correct the fault. We can do the same with our thoughts. It often helps to write them down and to practise replacing negative thoughts with positive thoughts when you are relaxed so they become automatic when you are in troubling situations. For example someone who is afraid of authority could practise: 'I don't need to be afraid of people in charge any longer. I am not a child now, I am safe, my confidence is growing etc.'

Choose any of the statements below that you feel are appropriate for you and add others that would be helpful. Write them down on postcards or pieces of paper.

(1) This crazy need to talk all the time means I am uptight and need to relax more.
(2) I will be patient with myself, I will be in charge again.
(3) Am I making this panic worse – am I hungry, breathing badly, etc? Put this card in several places: the fridge, bathroom mirror, on the television set, etc.
(4) *This card should go by the telephone.* Don't moan on and on – you know how stupid you feel afterwards.
(5) This is not my normal behaviour. It will go. I have everything I need inside myself to get better. Every day in every way I am getting better and better. I am a wonderful person, I deserve good health.

Have you identified which fear is dragging you down? Some common ones are: death, authority, injury, illness, growing old, being alone, failure, responsibility, personal relationships, sexuality.

Negative thoughts
Do some of your wayward thoughts also come from unrealistic expectations of how you or other people should behave? Have they crept up on you and are now so strong that they are affecting your life?

What are your expectations of others? How often are your demands unreasonable: I must be loved all the time/If they don't do as I say then they don't love me/If he does not notice when I'm tired, or when my shoes are worn out, then he can't love me/If she does not agree with everything I say then she is against me/I need total commitment in a relationship (does this mean total control?)

What are your expectations of yourself? If I lose my temper no-one will love me/If I don't look my best he will not love me/If I don't do everything she wants she will leave me/If I don't get good grades she will not love me/If I don't go home

75

for Christmas she will think I don't love her/I must not be seen to be wrong/I must not show weakness.

Can you have too much reassurance and support?   Ill people often need to be dependent for a time, but if this carries on too long it can stop them recovering – a similar effect to prolonged drug therapy. The strain of having to uphold a nervous person for long periods can also have a serious affect on the health of the relatives.

People dependency

People who are trapped by fearful or negative thoughts often seek constant reassurance. This affords only temporary relief and the sufferer wants more and more. This could be termed reassurance neurosis or people dependency. This happens not only in the therapeutic situation, but also in personal relationships. Some people become so dependent on their partner they cannot bear them to leave their side for a minute. This often puts a great strain on the marriage. The sufferer thinks only of how fearful they are and even insists that the partner stays awake if they cannot sleep. Sometimes the sufferer refuses to be in the house alone and the partner has to arrange a 'babysitter'.

If you feel your partner is being hard on you it is much better to say so even if you risk their tears or anger. It is not realistic or helpful to take it all and say nothing no matter how sympathetic you feel.

It is also very important not to let the sufferer talk endlessly about how they feel. Insist that they only talk about symptoms at certain times, say for ten minutes after dinner. They will be very angry at first and say you are unfeeling. Point out to them that they need to reach out to normality – it won't just land in their lap.

Treatment for people dependency   The cognitive therapist would encourage people to avoid seeking external sources of reassurance, teaching them the importance of reassuring themselves. Of course, it is unrealistic to expect sufferers to do this if you don't teach them to understand their nerves and how to relax.

Nothing can be more degrading than to need someone with you or to be on the phone constantly in order to get through the day. Use self-talk (see page 74).

15
Working with Your Body
– Relaxation

Working with the body to help your nerves

How tight muscles cause anxiety was discussed earlier (Chapter 3). You may think: I will just relax them and the anxiety levels will come down. Unfortunately, it is not as easy as that. The muscles are in the habit of tightening up, and you may not be aware of this until you realize you are walking around with your shoulders around your ears or your head pushed forward like a turtle. And here's the bad news; you are going to have to be constantly vigilant until your muscles are retrained.

It is an interesting comment (from Dr Joe McDonald) that panic attacks are easily induced in normal people by injecting lactate – a normal byproduct of overstressed muscle tissue.

Become aware of how you are using your body

The head

The head is heavier than is imagined; about 9.5 kg (about 1 to 1½ stones). If it is unbalanced it can affect the whole body. When you are anxious or depressed the muscles that run down the side of the neck (the sternomastoids) tend to become contracted or shortened, affecting the breathing, the head, neck, shoulders and all the way down the spine, through the pelvis, and even causing tension in the legs.

How to balance the head Sit on a chair with the spine straight, but not taut, look a few feet in front of you at the floor (if your eyes are down you cannot shorten the muscles at

78

the side of the neck); keep your shoulders *down*, now raise your eyes enough to comfortably look around the room – this is the balanced position for your head. The chin is pointing downwards not poking out in front. Whoever taught us to keep back straight, head up, shoulders back and chin up, did us a great disservice. It is an unnatural position for the head and spine.

The Alexander Technique

The Alexander Technique is one of the most successful methods of learning correct posture and how to move without tension.

It trains the body to move in a way that reduces stress and results in better posture. It can be helpful in many illnesses or after injury. The method is very gentle and concentrates on guiding the pupil's movements until he becomes aware of his bad habits. If you have a teacher near you it would be money well spent.

For more information see further reading, page 112.

Quick tension relief

This can be done anywhere – on a bus, in a friend's house, in the office. No-one needs to know what you are doing.

Sit with your head balanced as described above: drop your shoulders; imagine they are a coat hanger, and your body is a wet garment hanging from it. Check your head again, then shake your arms and place them palms upwards in your lap. Squeeze your thighs together, then let them fall back into position. Cross your ankles loosely and let the knees fall apart, or just place the feet flat on the floor.

Relaxation lying down – five or ten minutes

This is best on the floor, but can be done on the bed. Lying down increases the blood supply to the head (you will know this if you have ever had toothache), takes the force of gravity off the spine and gives the heart a rest. It takes a lot of energy to stay upright. Lying down also allows all your bones to fall into a natural position. We have seen that the relaxation response is more efficient after exercise. Here is a very quick exercise to do before lying down.

The wet dog exercise

Simply open your mouth and shake all over like a dog throwing water from his coat. Hold the wall or a chair and shake each leg. This is also a good exercise for people who are worried about shaking (through nerves) in public. It takes very much more energy to hold back the shaking than to have a really good shake. If you are out and are embarrassed by shaking, go into a lavatory and make yourself shake all over. After that you may not be able to shake even if you wanted to!

Make sure the room is not too cold or stuffy and have a blanket or coat near. Some people go very cold as they relax; others feel tingly and warm. A feeling of heaviness is usual, although some people say they feel light-bodied and light-headed. Ignore all these feelings. If you are very tense this routine should be as important in your day as brushing your teeth.

The tighten and let go method

It is better to avoid the tighten and let go method of relaxation, which asks you to tighten and relax each group of muscles in turn. If you are very tense, and particularly if you are coming off tranquillizers or alcohol, you can increase your discomfort by following this routine, as the muscles can go into spasm. It can be very uncomfortable if the wide muscle in the back (latissimus dorsi) contracts. You feel your back is arched and you cannot lie flat.

Longer relaxation session

Use the following routine:

(1) Lie on the floor, raise your head 7½ to 10 centimetres (3 or 4 inches) with something firm underneath like paperbacked books, bend your knees and have your feet flat on the floor (this is important if you have back trouble); if you have a good back and want to stretch out, do so after a couple of minutes.

(2) Take *one* deep breath through the nose. Imagine your whole body is being filled with air, then slacken the jaw and let the air slowly out through the mouth. Feel you are sinking through the floor.

(3) Mentally stroke each part of your body in turn and say to yourself three times each:

My right arm is heavy.
My left arm is heavy.
My right leg is heavy.
My left leg is heavy.
My whole body is heavy and comfortable.

Now go over the body again mentally stroking and this time saying:

My right arm is warm.
My left arm is warm, etc.

Finishing with:

My whole body is warm.

Now imagine a pure white light filling you with energy. Stretch, and wriggle fingers and toes. Turn onto your side then sit up. Wait for a moment before standing up slowly. This is a simple routine, but don't be surprised if your body does not respond too well at first. It may take some practice. You cannot force yourself into a relaxed state, that will make you tighten up even more. Just keep going through the exercise each day and it will come. You may notice that some muscles ache a little when you get up from the floor – they have had the benefit of an increased blood supply. This is a good sign. It means your body has let go and the joints have been allowed to go into a different position. When you were a child did you ever tie a string or rubber band around the end of your finger? The end goes numb. When you take the band off the blood rushes back and the finger can ache for a few seconds. This is what has happened in your muscles.

Using your body without tension – be aware

What am I doing with my head and neck?

Am I holding my head on one side?
Am I in the turtle position?
Am I pulling it back and sticking my chin up?
Do I strain my neck by turning it repeatedly to one side?
Do I have to turn it to watch TV, etc.?
Do I chew only on one side?

What am I doing with my shoulders?

Are my shoulders around my ears?
Is one shoulder higher than the other?
Am I curving one or both shoulders towards the front of my
   body?
Am I fiercely gripping: my pen, the steering wheel, the
   iron, my tools, my knitting needles etc.?
Am I pulling my shoulders up or holding my head on one
   side when I talk, wash dishes, travel, etc.?
Are my arms tightly folded over my chest? (We do this to
   protect us from the outside world and to keep our hurts
   and fears to ourselves.)
Are my fists clenched tightly all the time?
Am I pulling my thumb into an unnatural position?
Do I press my arms fiercely to my sides?

Am I afraid to really use my breathing muscles?
Am I tightening my stomach? – this is the cause of a great
   many problems.

When a doctor is examining a patient with an inflamed
appendix, the sufferer contracts his muscles over the sore
place to protect it from the pressure of the doctor's fingers.
This is called *guarding*. We do the same with our emotional
pain.

Gut feelings

The solar plexus is a collection of nerves just below the
diaphragm near the stomach and liver. This area is often
called the seat of the emotions. Think of some of the
expressions we use: gut feelings, I can feel it in my gut, he
dealt me a body blow, hitting below the belt, he got me in the
solar plexus. Tension in the abdomen can cause ulcers,
constipation and period problems.

*If you want a healthy inside you will have to let go of these
muscles.*

It is necessary to work on all the muscles, but the muscles of
the abdomen are particularly important because they also
affect the breathing. We shall see in Chapter 16 how vital it is
to breathe correctly.

Exercise for the solar plexus   When you are lying on the floor
or bed:

Imagine your stomach is the sea and on it is a boat with a
blue sail. Lift the boat up on a large wave, breathing in
through your nose, slowly but not deeply. Let the boat fall
as you breathe out. Just do this once, and don't worry if
your heart bumps a little.

Now with the lightest touch possible, rub your stomach
60 times in a clockwise direction. This is a helpful exercise
for people with a lot of wind.

What am I doing with my lower body?

Am I tensing my thighs because I have a fear of not making the lavatory in time?

Am I tightening up the muscles in the pelvic floor because I don't want to admit to sexual feelings?

Am I tightening up my legs when I walk because I wear the wrong shoes or because I really don't want to go out?

Using the body symmetrically

When you have discovered where you are holding your tension the next step is to work out how much the way you are moving is aggravating or indeed causing the problem. Make sure you use both sides of the body. For instance, don't always carry shopping on the same side or reach up to cupboards with the same arm.

It's worth taking care of your muscles because nervous people cannot even relax during sleep and often complain of aching and stiffness all over. They wake even more tired than when they went to bed.

Massage

If muscles are contracted with tension not only are they denied essential nutrients, but the waste products from metabolism (how the body uses food) are not flushed out and carried away. This builds up in the form of crystals rather like soap building up in laundry which is not adequately rinsed. This is why you can feel pain when someone is massaging your shoulders. When the muscle is pressed onto the bone the crystals can be felt. If the muscles are not moved the aching and stiffness will persist. Exercise will increase circulation and help to disperse the crystals, but you will get quicker results if you use massage as well. This does not have to be done by a professional. Anyone can do simple massage and if you watch the following points you cannot do any harm:

Do not massage over broken skin or varicose veins.
Do not press deeply into an inflamed muscle; use a very
  light touch.
Do not massage the front of the body, neck, breasts and
  stomach.

As long as you have followed these rules, try to turn your
mind off, relax and let your hands do the work. People who
have been tense for a long time are very surprised they can
feel so much more comfortable around the neck and
shoulders after even a short massage.

There are a few people who are anxious about relaxing
their shoulders, fearing they will 'go to pieces' or fall over
without the support of their 'armour'.

Working on the neck and shoulders

You do not need to know the person you are working with,
and in fact it is often better if you don't.

If you massage regularly either for a friend or in a group
your fingers will soon become sensitive to the feeling of the
muscles before and after a session.

Instructions for the sufferer   Some people (usually those who
have cared for others all their lives) find it very difficult to
allow their partner to help. Just *be* without worrying. Imagine
you are a rag doll. Your helper is not in the least interested in
whether your jumper came from Marks and Spencer or how
long it is since you washed your hair. She is interested in your
discomfort and how she can help.

Instructions for the helper   Be as relaxed as you can; let your
breath out as you drop your shoulders; feel the desire to help
your partner. Make sure her back is straight but slack, press
her shoulders down and check the position of her head.

(1) Support her forehead with one hand and move the

muscles of the scalp just as if you were washing her hair with the other.

(2) Continue to support the forehead; massage quite firmly at the base of the skull using the thumb and fingers to make small circular movements.

(3) Now move onto the back of the neck using the thumb and index finger on either side of the neck bones, again using a circular movement.

(4) Place your hands over the shoulders and use the thumb or heel of the hand to knead the muscles in a circular motion; ask if there are any places needing extra attention.

(5) Put one arm across the top of your partner's chest and encourage her to relax forward onto it. With the other hand continue massaging down the side of (but not on) the bones of the spine. Work in a similar fashion around the shoulder blade. Use the other arm and repeat for other side of spine.

(6) Stand in front of your partner, pick up the wrist and shake the hand letting it flop (unless there is pain in the joint), and ask her to imagine a wet sweater on the washing line. You will feel the arm become heavier when she thinks 'heavy'. Give the arm a little shake then do the same for the other hand and arm.

(7) Stand behind your partner, support the head against your chest and stroke the brow with both first fingers from the centre outwards.

(8) Finish off by stroking lightly and rapidly from the head down the back and then down the arms and hands.

Sometimes people are quite sleepy after a head and neck massage. Your partner might need a short rest before helping you.

It is a great help if a very tense person can have a massage daily. The therapeutic value of massage is becoming more recognized in this country. Aromatherapy, massaging with the essential oil of plants, has also been proved to have a beneficial effect on the nervous system (see further reading, page 112).

Getting the circulation going

When the fireman is fighting the fire his adrenalin levels are very high, but because he is so active he is burning off the excess. He can relax when his work is finished. Some people are so anxious they are afraid to move thinking they must reserve their energy just to get through the day; others say: 'I get enough exercise; I'm so wound up I rush around like a scalded cat.' Rushing around in a constant state of tension is almost as bad as not having any exercise; the adrenalin levels are not worked off by the effort because they are continually being topped up by tension.

If you are depressed get moving

If you are very depressed you might have so little energy that it is difficult to drag yourself from the bed to the chair; recovery will be much quicker if you start moving. It will be a terrible effort at first, but it will not harm you.

Exercises sitting on a chair

(1) Balance your head (see page 78), take one deep breath lifting your shoulders as you do so; open your mouth as you let the breath out and drop your shoulders. Feel like a pricked balloon.
(2) Breathe normally, lift the shoulders towards the ears and let them drop eight times.
(3) Keeping the arm limp, circle each shoulder in a clockwise direction eight times, and then try doing them together.
(4) Stretch both arms to the ceiling without straining, and let them fall loosely towards the floor.
(5) Stretch out the fingers, then draw eight circles each way with the forefingers.
(6) To exercise the legs draw the same circles with each big toe in turn.
(7) If you are not too tired, stand up and do any loose swinging movement you can think of.
(8) Finish with the wet dog shake.

Don't let it stop there: see how many gentle stretching exercises you can incorporate in your daily routine. For example, walk upstairs on your toes to stretch the backs of your legs, reach up to shelves with both hands, hold the stretch then relax. Do loose swinging movements, running on the spot, or the wet dog shake, when you are waiting for the kettle to boil. Before getting into the bath hold the side and bend your knees a few times; rotate your ankles or massage your hands as you watch television.

Building these movements into your daily routine is useful if you do not feel up to swimming, walking, yoga etc. Remember what happens to your circulation if you don't move.

16

Hyperventilation

Hyperventilation or overbreathing is breathing in a rapid, shallow way using the upper chest, instead of the abdomen. Breathing this way produces more oxygen than the body needs and the result is a fall in carbon dioxide levels in the blood. This causes a multitude of symptoms which can mimic most known diseases. It can complicate the picture where there is organic disease and it can also be the cause of endless fruitless investigations: neurological tests, heart tests, barium meals, etc.

How hyperventilating affects the body

Since the normal functioning of every system in the body depends on the correct amounts of oxygen and carbon dioxide circulating in the blood, it is easy to see why this 'unbalanced blood' causes such havoc. Although formerly it was thought that anxiety caused hyperventilation it is now known that it can be the other way round. L. C. Lum, Consultant Chest Physician, Papworth Hospital in his article on hyperventilation (Lum, 1981, see further reading, page 112) states that Rice (1950) turned this concept upside down and said that the anxiety was a result of the symptoms and also *that patients could be cured by eliminating faulty breathing.* Lewis (1964) *identified the role of anxiety as a trigger, rather than the prime cause* (my italics).

In another paper on hyperventilation Lum (1987, see further reading, page 112) also states: 'It now must be recognized as a major factor in many neuroses, particularly *panic disorder* and *phobic states*' (my italics).

Symptoms of hyperventilation

General exhaustion
Aching muscles
Panic attacks
Feelings of unreality
Depersonalization
Dizziness
Faintness
Irritability
Depression
Freefloating anxiety
Poor memory
Lack of concentration
Shortness of breath; need to take occasional deep breaths; sighing
Tingling hands and feet
Difficulty in swallowing

Pain in chest
Pain in neck and shoulders
Burping (sometimes bringing fluid with it)
Irritable bowel – wind distension
Allergies
Disturbed sleep
Distorted vision
Increased sensitivity to light and sound
Ringing in ears (tinnitus)
Increased effect of alcohol
Decrease in pain sensation

I think you would agree that this is a familiar list.

Recognizing hyperventilation

It is easy to recognize *severe* hyperventilation: erratic, noisy, rapid breaths where the chest is heaving and the abdomen is barely moving. The person feels the need to take an occasional deep breath and often finds it difficult to breathe out. Sighing at intervals seems to relieve this.

Chronic hyperventilation is not easy to identify because there is nothing dramatic to see or hear: quiet, shallow rapid breaths with most of the movement from the upper chest.

Often people are very unwilling to accept that their breathing pattern is causing their symptoms: 'My breathing has always been like this, how could it possibly be making me feel so ill.'

Sometimes during a consultation a doctor will encourage his patient to speed up his breathing; the rapid return of his symptoms – tingling, panic etc. – soon convinces him of the source of his troubles.

How one develops the habit of hyperventilating

There are several triggers: tension, depression, chest troubles, stuffy nose, allergies, wearing tight clothes or a spinal brace, folding arms across chest, physical pain, trying to hold in emotional pain.

Become aware of your breathing pattern

It will take time, probably several weeks, for your better breathing to become automatic, so be patient with yourself. To time your breathing rate look at a watch or clock with a second hand after you have been at rest for about ten minutes. Breathing in and out is one breath: see how many times you do this in 30 seconds then double it; this will give you the rate you are breathing per minute. If it is sixteen or more you would be wise to follow the exercises below. If you find it difficult to count your breaths, ask a family member to do it when you are unaware of what they are doing. If you find the exercises a bit boring, you could perhaps listen to a favourite programme on the radio while doing them. But *do* them – the results will be worth it.

Breathing exercises

These should be slow and gentle not deep and vigorous. Make the time to do two half-hour sessions daily. If you are having severe symptoms, panic or agoraphobia, a quick five minutes here and there is not enough. The best times are after breakfast and before the evening meal. Sit comfortably in the chair or better still lie on the floor or bed, and loosen tight clothing. As you become more skilled you will be able to do this anywhere, even, for instance, standing in a queue.

(1) Place one hand on your stomach and one on your chest. The hand on your chest should stay as still as possble. The hand on your stomach will go up and down as you breathe.
(2) Breathe out through your nose (don't force it), and let your stomach fall gently as you do so.
(3) Breathe in through the nose letting the stomach rise. Try to make the outward breath longer than the inward breath.
(4) Gradually train yourself to breathe between eight and twelve times per minute.

The aim is to breathe *slowly* lifting the abdomen. If you breathe too deeply you can become lightheaded or your heart may bump a little. This shows how not only low carbon dioxide levels but also a rapid change in these levels can cause symptoms. This is nothing to worry about, but if you get in a muddle take a rest and start again.

Panic attacks – using breathing to cope

If your attitude is, 'I will die, be sick, faint, wet myself etc., if I don't fight this panic attack,' you will encourage more attacks. It will become a trigger for stimulating more adrenalin, and thus more fear. If you teach your body to give the correct messages to your brain, you can break this chain reaction. If your thoughts are panic, panic, panic, they need to be followed by breathe, breathe, breathe – slow it down.

First aid for panic attacks
Since the main cause of the symptoms is too much oxygen

buzzing around in you, the aim is to cut it down as quickly as possible. Let your breath out in a long sigh and cup your hands around your nose and mouth to stop you taking in too much oxygen and crowding out the carbon dioxide.

If you are at home you could place a paper – never plastic – bag around your nose and mouth. Do not *blow* or breathe deeply into the bag – just let the breaths come, they will slow down naturally as you get your own carbon dioxide back from the air in the bag. You can also slow the breathing by splashing cold water on the face or putting cold cloths or ice packs over the cheeks and nose. It does not need to be an ice pack; a packet of frozen peas wrapped in a teatowel, for example can be very useful.

If breathing is the first thought, what next? This should be: eat or drink something sweet as soon as possible. Chapter 17 explains the importance of maintaining a steady level of sugar in the blood, and how eating sugar is only a first-aid measure for panic and should be followed by a meal and a rest.

17

Hypoglycaemia (Low Blood Sugar) and Nerves

What is hypoglycaemia?

Hypoglycaemia or low blood sugar is an abnormally low level of glucose in the blood. The food we eat is turned into glucose by the digestive system and we use the energy it produces to nourish our bodies, rather like putting petrol in a car.

Some people think if they eat lots of sugary foods they will be full of energy and the level of glucose (sugar) in their blood will stay normal. This chapter shows that the opposite is true, and it is necessary to cut down on these foods if you have nervous problems.

Hypoglycaemia is the opposite to diabetes, a disorder where the pancreas fails to produce the chemical called insulin. Insulin enables us to burn the food we eat to produce energy. The reverse is so in hypoglycaemia. The pancreas is overstimulated, usually because of nervous exhaustion and produces too much insulin. This causes the food we eat to be burned up too quickly and we cannot maintain the levels of blood glucose necessary to function normally.

The results are unpleasant physical effects such as palpitations and feeling faint, and because the brain cannot store glucose there are also unpleasant brain effects such as anxiety, depression, panic attacks and neurotic behaviour.

Is hypoglycaemia an illness?

Hypoglycaemia is not an illness, although there is increasing evidence to show that if it goes unchecked it can predispose you to some chronic illnesses, such as arthritis, ulcers, migraine, allergies, diabetes. It is common for a person with

94

hypoglycaemia to have a family history of these conditions.

But hypoglycaemia can be easily cured. All you have to do is revise your eating habits and perhaps slow down.

The most common symptoms of hypoglycaemia

Identifying symptoms and treating this problem has changed the lives of many, many people. Their panic attacks have gone, they are no longer tired, their concentration has returned and the craving for sugary foods, bread and/or alcohol has disappeared.

Blurred vision	Asthma
Headaches	Indigestion
Fainting	Chest pain
Epilepsy	Palpitations
Migraine	Feelings of inner trembling
Drowsiness	Overacid stomach
Jaundiced appearance	Overweight
Irritability	Food cravings
Poor concentration	Excessive smoking
Panic feelings	Allergies
Lack of coordination	Premenstrual tension
Alcoholism	Lack of sex drive
Hyperactivity	Cold hands and feet
Freefloating anxiety	Stiff muscles
Depression	Stiff joints

Other: feelings of inner trembling, being very dull in the mornings, feeling weak and confused mid-morning or mid-afternoon; wanting something sweet about an hour after main meals, waking between 2 and 3 am feeling hungry and anxious.

Of course many of the above symptoms can be caused by

other conditions. If you do not improve on the diet discussed later in this chapter, then you are unlikely to have a low blood sugar problem and it would be sensible to see your doctor.

Causes of hypoglycaemia

All the following can be causes: exhausted nerves, underfunction of the pituitary, thyroid, or adrenal glands; severe continuous muscular work; skipping meals, eating too much carbohydrate (sugar, sweets, chocolate, cakes, biscuits, bread), drinking alcohol or sweet drinks; taking drugs including caffeine, cigarettes, street drugs, the pill, steroids, tranquillizers, sleeping pills and beta-blockers. *Please note*: Always consult your doctor about cutting down or stopping prescribed drugs.

You can see from this list that it is relatively easy to disturb your blood sugar levels and because of this it is a very common problem indeed. It is also on the increase because of the growing numbers of pills swallowed and the amount of junk food eaten. Because the symptoms can be so dramatic it is often mistaken for more serious conditions, and in the same way as those with symptoms of hyperventilation, people are often subjected necessarily to a lot of tests.

It could be argued that every emotion has a physical 'twin', like hyperventilation it is another chicken-and-egg situation. Does the hypoglycaemia follow the exhausted nerves or is it the other way around? There is a great deal of evidence to show that it is much more usual for the physical changes to *precede* the emotional changes (mood swings, panic attacks, etc.), and if you think about this it makes more sense this way round. A disturbance in metabolism (body chemistry) is bound to cause personality changes.

Hypoglycaemia as a cause of panic attacks

Panic attacks are by far the most distressing symptoms of hypoglycaemia. This is how they happen:

The digestion of well-balanced meals keeps the blood sugar stable. In the absence of food the blood sugar falls and in order to keep our nervous system, muscles etc. functioning we have to call on our 'reserve tank', the glucose that is stored in the liver. The stomach cries 'Help the tank is empty', and the brain responds by sending a chemical messenger (yes, adrenalin, of course) to release the stored food (glucose) in the liver. Unfortunately as we have seen throughout this book too much adrenalin causes many unpleasant feelings, including panic attacks.

People are often very stubborn about accepting that they are causing their panic attacks by the way they're eating, or not eating. They also find it difficult to grasp that if they eat a high refined carbohydrate diet (lots of sweet foods, cereals, white bread, etc.) it can often be worse than missing a meal.

Some reasons

In Chapter 16 on hyperventilation we said that the carbon-dioxide level in the blood does not need to be way below normal for severe symptoms such as panic to develop; a sudden drop, even if it doesn't go below normal, can cause big trouble. It is the same with blood sugar levels; the *change* is the important factor. It is well documented that full-scale panic attacks and other symptoms can occur when the level is only on the lower end of the normal scale.

If you eat sugary foods, particularly when you are very hungry, the pancreas (which is already jittery and in top gear) pushes out more insulin than is necessary to cope with the sugar. The result is a rapid drop in blood sugar levels followed by a flood of adrenalin.

Some examples

June came in to the group session very tearful, saying she had just had a panic attack and it could not have been low blood sugar because she had stopped for lunch. When it was revealed that lunch was toast and a cream cake with two cups of black

97

coffee and a cigarette, the other group members could see what she had done. They helped her to see the pattern of her attacks. Thursday nights, Friday mornings and Sunday early evening. On Thursdays she has a night out with the girls, two gins and tonics followed by coffee and cake. During the week her evening meal is a 'proper meal', but on Sundays she has tea (sandwiches, scones, pies and cakes) with her mother. When she changed to one glass of dry white wine with cheese and crispbreads for Thursday evening, and a tuna salad and wholemeal bread instead of her usual Sunday tea, her panic attacks disappeared.

Note: If you make your blood sugar unstable it may not catch up with you until the next day or the middle of the night.

Julian had been having panic attacks for seven months. They started when he gave up smoking. He was very keen to try the low blood sugar way of eating because he already suspected missing meals was the trigger for his migraine. After four weeks he was confident he had found the cause of his trouble. He had only suffered three panic attacks; they were much milder than the ones he had previously experienced and two were after drinking beer and postponing his evening meal. His headaches had improved too.

Who is likely to have a hypoglycaemia problem?

Everyone will experience some degree of hypoglycaemia sometime in their lives. Have you ever seen an irritable, tearful young child become happy and relaxed as soon as he/ she has eaten, or felt your mind clear and the shaky feeling inside leave you, after you have a mid-morning break? A large part of the misery of a hangover is also due to low blood sugar.

Slimmers, athletes and nervous people are most likely to have severe symptoms of hypoglycaemia.

Addiction and hypoglycaemia

Many drugs including alcohol, cigarettes, tranquillizers and sleeping pills, artificially raise the blood sugar levels. When the level of the drug in the blood drops, the blood sugar also falls. There is often a confusion between symptoms of drug withdrawal and hypoglycaemia because they both include headache, anxiety, depression, shaking etc. While it is difficult to separate the symptoms, it is certainly *very clear that people withdrawing from drugs who keep to a hypoglycaemic eating plan, not only dramatically reduce their withdrawal symptoms, but are also much more likely to complete withdrawal and not feel the need to turn to other substances.* For example, people withdrawing from alcohol often turn to tranquillizers and vice versa.

It is very important for people in withdrawal who are from families where there are other hypoglycaemia problems (asthma, arthritis, allergy etc.) to follow the hypoglycaemic eating plan. It is also wise to start the diet three or four weeks *before* you intend to stop smoking, drinking or before you cut down the dose of tranquillizers or sleeping pills.

The hypoglycaemic diet

The following plan will keep blood sugar levels stable. *Note*: If your doctor has already given you a diet to follow consult him before you change to this one.

Principles of the diet

The aim is to avoid foods and substances that are quickly absorbed to minimize rapid changes of glucose levels in the blood.

Carbohydrates

Avoid or cut down to a minimum refined carbohydrates: these include sugar, sweets, chocolate, white bread, white flour, cakes, biscuits, pastry, alcohol, sweet drinks, junk foods.

Eat non-refined carbohydrates (complex): these include whole grain cereals – wheat, oats, barley, rice, rye, millet.

Give up processed breakfast cereals and make your own muesli from whole oats, nuts, seeds (sunflower, pumpkin or sesame are all very nutritious) and a little dried fruit (sultanas, apricots etc.). If you are used to eating 'plastic bread' you will love the taste of wholegrain brown bread, and if you normally eat brown bread make sure it is wholegrain.

Protein

Animal protein: meat, fish, poultry, cheese, eggs, milk, yogurt.
Vegetable protein: nuts, seeds, peas, beans, lentils and possibly small amounts in all vegetables.

There is always a lot of argument about how much protein should be included in any diet. The early diets for low blood sugar were very high in protein. Eating this way certainly controls the blood sugar, but more recent research has shown that the body does not like too much concentrated protein, and blood sugar levels can be kept steady on smaller amounts particularly if plenty of raw vegetables are included.

Vegetables and fruit

Eat large quantities of vegetables. These will supply you with essential minerals and vitamins and provide roughage. Some people have become overanxious about roughage – bran with everything. This is not a good idea, as it can irritate the bowel and hinder the absorption of some minerals. Eating vegetables is a better way to get roughage.

Eat lots of fresh fruit. Although fruit contains quite a lot of sugar, it is in a different form (fructose); it does not need insulin for its digestion, therefore it is an ideal food to help slow down the pancreas.

Fat

People also tend to worry too much about cholesterol levels. Next time you are about to spread your bread with some tasteless margarine (which is probably full of nasty additives anyway), remind yourself that worrying and not eating raw vegetables and fruit can be just as damaging as moderate amounts of butter. Also remember that some foods, including onions, garlic, apples and olive oil, actually *lower* cholesterol levels. Olive oil is also wonderful for the immune system, the body's defence against disease.

The diet

As soon as you get up or in bed	Small glass of unsweetened juice 100 ml (4 oz), half a grapefruit or medium orange
Breakfast	More fruit juice or fruit and choose from: Cooked breakfast: grilled bacon, fish, eggs, baked beans, cold ham, cottage cheese or any protein dish, plus any vegetable, such as tomatoes or mushrooms; one slice of wholemeal bread, two crispbreads, rice cakes etc. with butter or margarine *or* Whole oat porridge sweetened with a few sultanas or muesli made from whole cereals, nuts, seeds (pumpkin, sunflower etc.) or plain yogurt with

101

	fresh fruit and nuts. You can flavour this with spices: cinnamon, ginger, crushed cardamom. Weak tea with milk if desired or one cup weak coffee
Two hours after breakfast	Snack: fruit, yogurt, nuts, milk
Lunch	Any protein dish: hot or cold meat, fish, cheese, eggs, chicken, sardines, tuna, pilchards etc. or any lentil, bean or nut dish. All to be eaten with *lots of salad or vegetables*, one slice of wholemeal bread or two crispbreads
Two-and-a-half to three hours after lunch or earlier	Weak tea, milk, with crispbread with cottage cheese, paté or low sugar jam
Half to one hour before dinner	100 ml (4 oz) fruit juice
Dinner	Same as lunch plus fruit
Supper	Crispbread and butter with cottage cheese, etc., weak tea, herb tea etc.

This diet plan might look like a lot of food, but there is no need to eat large quantities – small and often is the rule.

Try not to make a new way of eating another of life's stresses. As your symptoms improve you can add treats like a glass of dry white wine or a piece of cake. Many people really crave sugar at first and experience aches and pains and other withdrawal feelings. These go after a few days. Other people also say they have more energy than they have had for years eating this way. And when they try to go back to their old eating habits after their nerves have improved they often find they have lost their taste for junk food and miss the clean taste of vegetables and fruit.

Dos and don'ts

Don't skip meals.
Eat regularly.
Avoid sugary foods and drinks, white flour.
Cut down on caffeine, cigarettes and alcohol.
Always have protein in your breakfast.
Never eat a starch-only meal (bread, cake, cereal).

Being overweight

If you are overweight you should lose weight with this eating plan because it does not include a lot of carbohydrate. If this does not happen you could try excluding *all* grains or cut down on the quantities at each meal, but continue to eat at the same times. Remember you will not lose weight by going for long periods between meals. This will make you crave all the foods you should not have. If your weight is still not coming down after a few weeks see your doctor; there may be another reason for your overweight, such as an underactive thyroid.

Being underweight

Some people who have had a high sugar and fat diet lose weight at first on this eating plan before starting to gain. If you want to put on weight eat more potatoes, bread, rice and milk drinks *and* slow down. Your weight should improve. A persistent weight loss should always be reported to your doctor, but do give yourself time for your body to adjust to this way of eating.

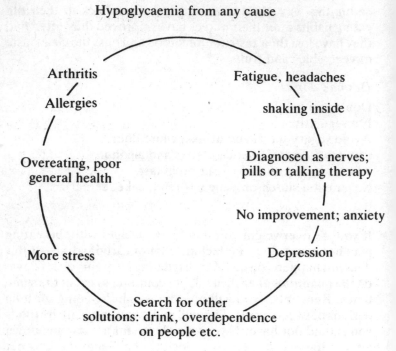

The circle of misdiagnosed hypoglycaemia

18

Quick References to Combat Depression and Anxiety

Depression

(1) *Move*. Get your circulation going.
(2) Don't lie in bed; get up same time each day (9 am at the latest).
(3) Even if you can't do much, do *something*; you can finish it the next day.
(4) Eat good food at regular meals.
(5) Try to walk 20 minutes in the brightest part of the day; don't wear your dark glasses. If you can't face walking sit by an open window.
(6) Build up exercise; force leaden limbs to move; use breathing exercises.
(7) Go to bed early.

Every day in every way you are getting better and better.
Believe it – it works!

Anxiety

(1) *Slow down*.
(2) Have a short relaxation before eating – regular meals, good food.
(3) Rest in the middle of the day.
(4) Use breathing exercises.
(5) Have plenty of fresh air, and outdoor exercise if possible.
(6) Use self-talk.
(7) Go to bed early.

PART THREE
What About the Spirit?

19

What About the Spirit?

A cheerful heart is good medicine but a crushed spirit dries up the bones

Proverbs 22

I have left this chapter until last, not because I feel it is least in importance, but because I expected some might say: 'If this is going to be God-talk, I don't want to know.'

My lack of confidence on this subject also made me hesitate. I have little formal knowledge and feel ill-equipped to write about spiritual health. It would be simple if I could tell you this as easily as I have said above: eat this way and you will feel better, or breathe this way and you will cut down panic attacks; all I can do is share with you what I feel and what I have seen.

I apologize to readers of other faiths that I can only speak of the Christian path to God because this is all I know, and even this much more with my heart than with my head.

During the experience of nervous illness (or indeed, any illness) many people become aware of something beyond themselves and the world in which they live. They renew their faith in God or discover His love for the first time, and often, even when they can be physically still quite low, they seem to glow with something beyond a clear skin and healthy hair. All I can think is, this is due to a peaceful spirit, one that is secure in the knowledge of where it is going.

What is the Spirit?

I believe this is the part of us that defies death: our God-spark; our essence; our soul; our personality; the part of us that is uniquely *us*; the part that chooses which path to take;

negative, or positive, the part that houses the love and learning we carry into the next world.

What keeps us from God?

Anxiety, depression, and drugs can all stop us growing spiritually. Lack of forgiveness and hanging on to righteous indignation (we often do this to bolster a low self-esteem) also prevent us from going forward. Some people distance themselves from God because they mistakenly believe they have to be 'good' or religious to have contact with Him. He accepts us exactly how we are and is always ready to forgive our mistakes. Real forgiveness brings great healing.

Sometimes early religious teaching, particularly the 'hellfire and damnation' variety can be very damaging. If this has been your experience try to let it go, and as you become real (see Chapter 7) you will see how very real God is too. He asks us to come to Him as little children. There is no need to make it complicated. Perhaps your prayer could be something like:

Lord, help me to see You through the fog of depression,
To hear You with ears ringing with anxiety,
And to accept only Love and learning endure and
All will be well in Your time, not mine.

This poem says the rest:

The New Casualty Officer

A youth, with bowed golden head walks across a battlefield
Manacled to him are his corpsed hurts
He has collected them from prenatal days
His mother's fears stung his budding limbs for
Even as a rosy blob he was twice as wise as she.

WHAT ABOUT THE SPIRIT?

A nurse walks past carrying a bowl of water,
She feels his pain, but knows he would not heed her words,
Over her shoulder she 'throws':
'Have you seen the New Casualty Officer?'
'Where is His tent?' the boys asks,
'You won't see it unless you raise your eyes,' she replies
    firmly.
His wounds were not cuts and abrasions; could anything help?
He thought of the many times before;
'We all feel like that at times, old man – take these pills
And if all else fails, have a chat with the psychiatrist.
I can give you his name.'
The cluttered desk between them was not the real divide.
'Old man' was right, for that was how his young bones felt.
The Man was waiting, calling him by his pet name, not his
    number.
He held him without touching, and silently counselled.
The boy knew he should have 'freaked' to use a word of his
    own
But did not, and instead, asked what he must do to be free.
Face your corpses, rage at them if you must, then with a
    kiss, forgive them and let them rest.
'Is that all?' replied the boy, astonished: 'No not all,' said
    the Wise Man.
Ask Me to stand by you while you do and say you would
    like me to stay.
The boy agreed and left.
He leapt to touch the branch of a tree as children escaping
    the classroom do.
He shouted to the others forming a queue:
'Hey, that New Chap is good.
He has done something to my eyes.'

Using his arms he weaved through the waist-high corn,
Conscious as he did so that he was making a path for the
    others.
How could joy come so suddenly?

Books, tapes and further information

Barlow, Wilfred, *The Alexander Principle*, Arrow 1975. To find your nearest qualified Alexander Teacher contact The Society of Teachers of the Alexander Technique, 10 London House, 266 Fulham Road, London SW10 9EL. Telephone: 071 351 0828.

Blackwood, John, and Fulder, Stephen, *Garlic – Nature's Original Remedy*.

Chaitow, Leon, *Candida Albicans: Is Yeast Your Problem?*, Thorsons 1987.

Davies, Stephen, and Stewart, Alan, *Nutritional Medicine*, Pan 1986.

Dawes, Belinda, and Downing, Damien, *Why M.E.?*, Grafton 1989. Clear and practical guidelines for coping with M.E. written by two doctors, one of whom is a sufferer from the disease. For further information on M.E. write to the M.E. Association, P.O. Box 8, Stanford le Hope, Essex SS17 8EX.

Dickson, Ann, *A Woman in Your Own Right: Assertiveness and You*, Quartet 1988.

Downing, Damien, *Daylight Robbery – The Importance of Sunlight to Health*, Arrow 1988.

Grant, Doris, and Joice, Jean, *Food Combining for Health*, Thorsons 1986.

Lewis, David, *Fight Your Phobia and Win*, Sheldon 1984.

Lum, L. C., 'Hyperventilation and anxiety state', *Journal of the Royal Society of Medicine, vol. 74* (January 1981).

— 'Hyperventilation Syndromes in Medicine & Psychiatry: a review', *Journal of the Royal Society of Medicine, vol. 80* (April 1987).

Powell, John, *Why am I Afraid to Tell You Who I Am*, Fontana 1975.

— *Why Am I Afraid to Love*, Argus 1978.

— *Unconditional Love*, Argus 1978.

Ramsay, Melvin, *Post-viral Syndrome – The Saga of the Royal Free Disease*, ME Association (see address above) 1988.

Stepping Out – Freedom From Minor Tranquillisers and Sleeping Pills, BBC. Available from Stepping Out, P.O. Box 7, London W3 6XJ.

Tisser, Maggie, *The Art of Aromatherapy*, Thorsons 1986. For further information on aromatherapy write to the International Federation of Aromatherapists, 46 Dalkeith Road, London SE21.

Trickett, Shirley, *Coming off Tranquillizers and Sleeping Pills*, Thorsons 1986.

Weekes, Claire, *Good Night, Good Morning*; *Moving to Freedom*; *Going on Holiday*; *Nervous Fatigue – Understanding and Coping with it*; *Hope and Help for Your Nerves*. These tapes and very useful leaflets on relaxation available from: Relaxation for Living, Dunesk, 29 Burwood Park Road, Walton on Thames, Surrey KT12 5LH.

Wright, Celia, *The Wright Diet*, Grafton 1989.

Index

Abreaction 59, 73
Addiction
  and hypoglycaemia 90
  to tranquillizers 55
Adrenalin levels 10, 16
Agoraphobia 16, 22–3
Alcoholism 95
Alexander Technique 79, 112
Allergies 60–3, 90, 95
  food 61
  chemical 61
Anxiety
  drug treatment for 55–7
  explained 6
  free-floating 90–5
  levels 10–13
  non-drug treatment for 58–9
  physical reasons for 60
  quick reference 105
  types of 37–9
Anxiolytics 56 *see also*
  Tranquillizers
Assertiveness 32–3
Attention-seeking 14

Barium meals 89
Behaviour
  aggressive 57
  neurotic 95
  of the hurt child 31
  therapy 23
Benzodiazepines 56–7
Body-mind interaction 60
Breakdown, nervous 49–54

Breathing
  difficulties 14, 90
  exercises 91
  patterns 91
  re-training 23
British Medical Journal 56

Cancer, fear of 15
Candida albicans 61–3
Candida Albicans: Is Yeast Your
  Problem? 62, 112
Carbohydrate 99
Catharsis 59, 73
Chest, tight 14
Chlordiazepoxide (librium)
  see Tranquillizers
Cognitive therapy 74
Coming off Tranquillizers and
  Sleeping Pills 3, 55
Committee on the Safety of
  Medicines 56
Communication, open and
  honest 34–6
Compulsions 14, 20–1
Concentration, lack of 4–24, 90
Co-ordination, lack of 95
Counselling 58–9
Crying 14
Cystitis 65

Depression
  agitated 44
  endogenous 42
  function of 8

manic 42, 45
masked 42–5
mixed 44
physical reasons for 60
psychotic 42
SAD (seasonal affective
    disorder) 45
treatments for 55–9
what does it feel like? 46
Depersonalization 90
Desensitization 22
Diarrhoea 14
Diazepam (valium) see
    Tranquillizers
Diet
    hypoglycaemic 99
    when overweight 103
    when underweight 103
Disorders
    affective 42
    glandular 60
    mood 56
    perceptual 56
    personality 57
Dizziness 14, 90
Doctor, going to 50–2

Ears, ringing in 14
Eating, compulsive 14
Epilepsy 95
Exercise
    'wet dog' 80
    for solar plexus 83
    in the chair 87

Flying, fear of 19
Food cravings 95
Fungal problems, see Candida

Guilt 39

Headaches 14
Heart
    bumping 14 see also
        Palpitations
Hyperactivity 14, 23, 24, 95
Hyperventilation 89–93
Hypnotics 56
Hypoglycaemia 94–104

Impotence 14
Insomnia 14, 24–6, 56
Investigations
    endless 89
    heart 89
    neurological 89
Irritability 14
Irritable bowel 62, 90

Lancet, The 23
Light treatment 59
Lithium 58
Lorazepam (ativan) see
    Tranquillizers
Low blood sugar see
    Hypoglycaemia
Lum, L.C. 89

MAOIs (monoamine-oxidase
    inhibitor) 58
Massage 84–6
ME (Myalgic
    encephalomyelitis) 63
Memory, poor 90
MIND (National Association
    for Mental Health) 49–50
Misdiagnosis 68–9
    circle of misdiagnosed
        hypoglycaemia 104

Muscles 90
  cramp 65
  tired 65
  working with 78–88
McDonald, Dr J.W. xi-xii, 78

National Health Service 3, 63
Nervous breakdown 49–54
Nervous symptoms 14, 65
Nervous system
  autonomic 9
  central 9
    parasympathetic 9–11, 12–13
    sympathetic 9–11
Neurosis 28–31, 61
Nitrazepam (mogadon) see
  Tranquillizers
Nutritional deficiencies 65
Nutritional Medicine 65, 112

Obsessions 14, 20, 57

Pain 64, 69
  emotional, 69
  stored, see Neurosis
Palpitations 95
Panic attacks 14, 16–20, 90, 92–3
Paranoia 14
People dependency 76–7
Phenothiazines 58
Phobias 14, 21–3

Relaxation 78–88

Royal Free Disease, see ME

SAD (Seasonal affective
  disorder) 59
Samaritans 16
Self-esteem 31
Self-talk 74
Sex drive, lack of 95
Solar plexus 83
Speech, rapid 14–15
Spirit, the 109–11
Stress 27–8
Suicidal feelings 14–16
Swallowing problems 14
Sweating, excessive 14

Thoughts
  negative 15, 24, 74–5
  positive 74
Tingling
  of hands and feet 90–1
Tinnitus 14
Tranquillizers 55, 59, 80, 99
  and phobias 23
  and ME 64
  and yeast infections 61
Tricyclic antidepressants 58

Weekes, Dr Claire 49, 113
Weight loss 14
Winter blues (SAD) 59
Withdrawal symptoms
  from antidepressants 58
  from tranquillizers 56